CVCBA
CHAMBER

Camp Verde Chamber Resource 2022-2023

Published by Glorybound Publishing
Camp Verde, Arizona
SAN 256-4564
Published in the United States of America
ISBN 9798836865849
Copyright data is available on file.
1st Edition
Hauser, Sheri, 1957-
  Camp Verde Chamber Resource 2022-2023/Sheri Hauser
   Includes biographical reference.
1. Arizona Business   2. Business Directory   I. Title

www.gloryboundpublishing.com
www.campverde.biz

Special thanks to the team who assisted with the compilation of the Camp Verde Chamber Resource. Paul Hauser and John Smoley were instrumental in tracking down hidden businesses. Colleen Elliot worked tirelessly to vet the businesses as they were located. Dana Donahue worked as a publisher compiling the the 2022-23 Edition adding additional businesses from the 2021 Edition. Entire project oversee Manager is Publisher, Sheri Hauser, Chamber Board Member and owner of Glorybound Publishing. This Resource is a great option to have at one's fingertips because it is a complete listing of all the local businesses registerd in Camp Verde. Chamber Members are flagged and have their logos. Advertising is for sale. See the chamber website for prices and ordering advertising.

Camp Verde Chamber Resource

2022-2023

Compiled By
Sheri Hauser

Glorybound Publishing
Camp Verde, Arizona
Released 2022

Camp Verde Chamber Resource

Table of Contents

Emergency

Abuse

National Sexual Assault Hotline. Free. Confidential. 24/7. Get the latest news on the work RAINN is doing every day to end sexual violence. From the legal definition of rape to the statute of limitation for a particular sex crime, where you live makes a difference. See our guide to the laws in your state. Hear from courageous survivors about what it means to tell their story and be believed, and the many paths they take to continue healing after sexual violence. National Domestic Violence Hot line 1−800−799−7233

Contact Information

Web Address
https://www.rainn.org/
Face Book URL
https://www.facebook.com/RAINN01/
Email: talk@rainn.org
Telephone # 1-800-799-7233

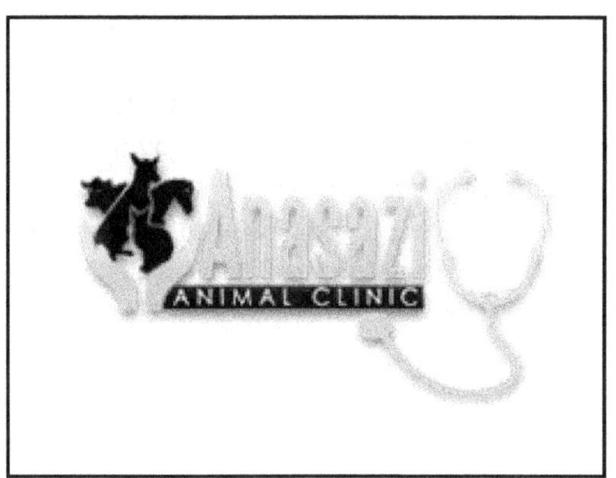

√Anasazi Animal Clinic

407 Az-260, Camp Verde, Az 86322
Anasazi Animal Clinic is a full service animal clinic and will take both emergency cases as well as less urgent medical, surgical, and dental issues, boarding and house calls. Dr. Gary Pollock is experienced in all types of conditions and treatments. Beyond first rate pet care, we make our clinic comfortable, kid-friendly, and a very calm environment so your pet can relax in the waiting room and look forward to meeting his or her own veterinarian.

Anasazi Animal Clinic has the technology to do most blood work in house in as little as 15 minutes with results as reliable as a reference laboratory. With this technology it will enables us to provide immediate and better care for your pet. We also offer the best in nutrition, we carry Hill's products, Science Diet and Prescription Diet foods and treats provide the best nutrition available for dogs and cats.

Contact Information

Web Address
http://www.anasazianimalclinic.com/
Face Book URL
https://www.facebook.com/Anasazi-Animal-Clinic-153485504677488/?ref=ts&fref=ts
Email: anasazianimalclinic@gmail.com
Telephone # 928-567-3807

Arizona Coalition To End Sexual and Domestic Violence

2700 N. Central Ave, Suite 1100
Phoenix, AZ 85004
News, resources, recent updated information, education, training.

Contact Information

Web Address
https://www.acesdv.org/
Face Book URL
Telephone # 602-279-2900
toll-free 1-800-782-6400

EMERGENCY

Arizona Department of Public Safety

999 Finnie Flat Road, Camp Verde, AZ 86322
The Arizona Department of Public Safety offers a wide variety of services to the public.
Public Services Include:

- Missing Children Search
- Sex Offender Compliance
- Concealed Weapons
- Fingerprint Clearance Card
- File a Commendation
- Licensing
- Courts & Tickets Information
- Claiming Personal Property
- Records Requests
- Report a Crime
- Submit a Tip (Silent Witness)
- Tow Truck Application
- Household Goods Enforcement

Enforcement Service Sections

- Chaplaincy Program Services
- Commercial Vehicle Enforcement
- DUI Enforcement
- Gang & Immigration Intelligence Team
- Enforcement Mission (GIITEM)
- Impaired Driving
- Move Over Law
- Scrap Metal Theft Database
- Student Transportation
- WANTED Fugitive Tips

Governmental Services

- Arizona Disposition Reporting System (ADRS)
- Arizona Department of Transportation (ADOT)
- Automated Fingerprint Identification
- Crime Lab Services
- Crime Victims Services
- Noncriminal Justice (NCJ) Compliance
- Tow Program
- Arizona Statewide Interoperability Coordinator SWIC

Contact Information

Web Address
https://www.azdps.gov/
Silent Witness:
https://www.azdps.gov/services/public/silent_witness
Face Book URL
https://www.facebook.com/Ariz.DPS
Telephone # 928-567-4257

Arizona Highway Patrol

Arizona Department of Public Safety (State Troopers)
999 Finnie Flat Rd #809, Camp Verde, AZ 86322

The Highway Patrol Division (HPD) is staffed by uniformed state troopers; they are highly recognizable by an all-tan uniform and Montana Peak (Smokey) hat. HPD is comprised of troopers assigned throughout the state who help fulfill the AZDPS mission of protecting human life and property by enforcing criminal and traffic law. Troopers patrol over 6,800 linear miles – which actually total 27,000 highway lane miles across 16 districts statewide and serve as the front line in deterring criminal activity along Arizona's highways. The division combines enforcement, training and public outreach to improve highway safety, while striving to reduce collisions and increase the efficiency of the highway transportation system. One of the responsibilities of HPD is to support the state of Arizona and its citizens by patrolling the Capitol districts both in Phoenix and Tucson.

HPD is composed of the following units:

- Analytical Unit
- Commercial Vehicle Enforcement (CVE)
- DUI Enforcement
- Metro Highway Patrol Bureau
- Northern Highway Patrol Bureau
- Roadside Motorist Assistance (RMA)
- Southern Highway Patrol Bureau
- Special Enforcement Bureau
- Traffic Operations Center (TOC)

EMERGENCY

Contact Information
Web Address
https://www.azdps.gov/organization/hpd
Face Book URL
https://www.facebook.com/Ariz.DPS
Telephone # 928-567-4257

____

Camp Verde Fire District Adm.
26 W. Salt Mine Road, Camp Verde, AZ 86322
Welcome to the Copper Canyon Fire and Medical District website; the newly minted agency responsible for providing fire suppression, emergency medical service, rescue, hazardous materials response, and fire prevention services to the communities of Camp Verde, McGuireville, Rimrock, and Lake Montezuma. We will be using this website, as well as press releases and social media to keep everyone informed of the proposed changes. We also look forward to addressing any concerns or comments about how we are doing in providing service to the community.
Contact Information
Web Address
https://ccfmd.az.gov/
Face Book URL
https://www.facebook.com/CopperCanyonFMD/
posts/50721406994479614
Email: kkrebbs@ccfmd.az.gov
Telephone # 928-567-9401

____

Camp Verde Marshal's Office
 646 South 1st Street, Camp Verde, Arizona 86322
Monday – Thursday
7:00 a.m. to 5:00 p.m.
Contact Information
Web Address
https://www.campverde.az.gov/departments/
marshal-s-office
Face Book URL
https://www.facebook.com/
Campverdemarshalsoffice/
Telephone # 928-554-8300

Coconino National Forest Red Rock Ranger District
8375 AZ-179, Sedona, AZ 86351
Get the scoop on the Red Rock Ranger District!

- Recreation Guide [PDF]
- Recreation Maps
- Red Rock Pass Information and find out where to get a Red Rock Pass
- Fee-free Days
- Road Status
- Forest Orders
- Buy a Red Rock Pass
- Red Rock Pass Program
- Drone Use Information
- Fossil Creek Recreation Info
- Dispersed Camping Guidelines
- Motorcycle Trail & Enduro Rides
- Leave No Trace

Popular Destinations
- Arizona Snowbowl
- C.C. Cragin Reservoir
- Lava River Cave
- Fossil Creek
- Oak Creek Canyon
- Sycamore Canyon
- Verde River
- Wet Beaver Wilderness

Contact Information
Web Address
https://www.fs.usda.gov/recarea/coconino/
recarea/?recid=54892
Face Book URL
https://www.facebook.com/CoconinoNF
Email: coconino_webmail@fs.fed.us
Telephone # 928-203-7500

____

Copper Canyon Fire & Medical

26B Salt Mine, Camp Verde, AZ 86322
Welcome to the Copper Canyon Fire and Medical District website; the newly minted agency responsible for providing fire suppression, emergency medical service, rescue, hazardous materials response, and fire prevention services to the communities of Camp Verde, McGuireville, Rimrock, and Lake Montezuma.

Contact Information

Web Address
https://ccfmd.az.gov/
Face Book URL
https://www.facebook.com/campverdefire
Email: rcook@ccfmd.az.gov
Telephone # 928-567-9401

Cottonwood Police Department

199 S. 6th Street, Cottonwood, AZ 86326
Divisions:
Patrol: The Patrol division oversees bicycle patrol, school safety officers, SWAT, and more. Support Services: Support services includes investigations, records, and the citizen police academy.

Contact Information

Web Address
http://cottonwoodaz.gov/328/Police-Department
Face Book URL
https://www.facebook.com/CityOfCottonwoodAZ
Email: rrodriguez@cottonwoodaz.gov
Telephone # 928-634-4246

√ Hope Women's Center

77 General Crook Trail, AZ 86322
We do this through a multitude of **FREE**, confidential services and programs which include:

- 1:1 Mentoring and Support Groups
- Parenting classes
- Life Skills and Faith Based Education Classes
- Grief Support and Celebrate Recovery
- Rise Above Abuse and Anger Management Classes
- Classes for birth moms with children in Foster Care or at risk of DCS removal
- Pregnancy Testing and Prenatal Classes
- ROSES Program for Pregnant Moms & Moms of Newborns (reducing Postpartum Depression)
- Specialized Maternal Mental Health support
- Childcare (0-5) for mothers attending Hope programs*
- Hope Heals - Crisis Counseling & Support
- Hope at Work - Job Skills Classes/Training
- Maternity Home for pregnant and parenting moms
- Points earned for programs can be used for Material Assistance such as utilities**, transportation, food, clothing, personal care items, household items, and baby/child products

Contact Information

Web Address
https://hopewomenscenter.org/
Face Book URL
https://www.facebook.com/abidematernityhome/
Email: Info@AbideMaternityHome.com
Telephone # 928-567-5433
928-713-7007 after hours
Pregnancy option hotline: 800-712-4357

EMERGENCY

Montezuma Rimrock Fire Department (Copper Canyon Fire Department)

26B Salt Mine, Camp Verde, AZ 86322
Welcome to the Copper Canyon Fire and Medical District website; the newly minted agency responsible for providing fire suppression, emergency medical service, rescue, hazardous materials response, and fire prevention services to the communities of Camp Verde, McGuireville, Rimrock, and Lake Montezuma.

Contact Information

Web Address
https://ccfmd.az.gov/
Face Book URL
https://www.facebook.com/campverdefire
Email: rcook@ccfmd.az.gov
Telephone # 928-567-9401

Montezuma Veterinary Services

298 W. General Crook Trail, Camp Verde, AZ 86322
We are a full-service animal hospital providing comprehensive healthcare services to pets in Camp Verde and the surrounding areas. Our veterinarians offer a wide variety of medical, surgical, and dental services in our veterinary clinic. We provide complete care for our patients. Our veterinary hospital is well equipped with advanced equipment and technology to provide the highest standard of care for your pet. Our facility has the equipment to provide comprehensive in-house testing for accurate diagnosis, digital x-ray, ultrasound, surgical suite, dental suite, pharmacy, and more.

Contact Information

Web Address
https://www.montezumavet.com/
Face Book URL
https://www.facebook.com/profile.php?id=100057350362374
Email: montezumaveterinary@gmail.com
Telephone # 928-567-5515

Northern Arizona Healthcare Immediate Care – Camp Verde

1298 Finnie Flat Rd, Camp Verde, AZ 86322
Immediate Care is a walk-in service where providers can treat all of the same conditions treated at an urgent care, but at a lower cost. Patients pay the same co-pay for an Immediate Care visit as they pay to see their primary care provider. Patients are seen by providers in order of greatest need. Same-day appointments will be on a walk-in basis only and not scheduled. The Camp Verde Campus also offers imaging and laboratory services on-site allowing Immediate Care providers access to these services to effectively and efficiently treat patients.

Conditions treated at Immediate Care include:

Abdominal pain	Cuts and lacerations
Allergies	Ear and eye infections
Back pain	Migraines
Bites and stings	Hypertension
Asthma	Nausea and diarrhea
Broken bones	Pneumonia
Bronchitis	Rashes and skin conditions
Minor burns	Sinus infections
Colds and flu	Sexually transmitted diseases
Strep throat	Urinary tract infections
Sports physicals	Camp physicals
Minor injuries	

Contact Information

Web Address
https://www.nahealth.com/immediate-care
Face Book URL
https://www.facebook.com/NAHVerdeValley/
Telephone # 928-639-5555

NextCare Urgent Care - Cottonwood

450 S Willard St #120, Cottonwood, AZ 86326
Hours: Mon-Fri 8A-6P, Sat-Sun 9A-5P
NextCare helps you get the care you need the moment you need it. Here are some of the things we treat at our location. Illness, Physicals, Immunizations & vaccinations, X-Rays, Injuries, Occupational Medicine. Covid-19 Testing, Antibody Testing, Alternative entrance for those experiencing COVID-19 symptoms. Insurance Accepted. We accept most major insurance companies. Here are some of the more commonly seen insurances accepted at this location. If you have questions about a specific insurance provider, please call (888) 381-4858 to check with our staff.

Insurance accepted: Aetna, Cigna, BCBA, Health Choice, Mercy Care, United Healthcare, Care 1st, Medicaid (HCCCS)

Contact Information

Web Address
https://nextcare.com/locations/az/cottonwood/
Face Book URL
https://www.facebook.com/NextCareUrgentCare/
Telephone # 928-634-2574

Poison Control

Contact Poison Control right away if you suspect a poisoning. Identify a pill, Poison and prevention information, poison statistics,Information on batteries. Get help online or on the phone. Help is available online with webPOISONCONTROL® or by phone at 1-800-222-1222. Both options are free, expert, and confidential. 24hr

Contact Information

Web Address
https://www.poison.org/
Telephone # 1-800-222-1222

Prescott National Forest Verde Ranger District Office

300 AZ-260, Camp Verde, AZ 86322
Recreation
Alerts & Notices
Passes & Permits
Maps & Publications
Land & Resource Management
Learning Center
News &Events

Prescott Dispatch Center
Prescott National Forest
Prescott Fire Center
2400 Melville Rd. Prescott AZ 86301
Phone: (928) 777-5610

Contact Information

Web Address
https://www.fs.usda.gov/detail/prescott/
home/?cid=fswdev3_009840
Telephone # 928-567-4121

Protection Orders

Welcome to AZPOINT, the Arizona Protective Order Initiation and Notification Tool. Through an interview in this portal, you can quickly fill out the forms that you need to ask for an Order of Protection at an Arizona court. IMPORTANT: There is NO FEE to use AZPOINT. AZPOINT is made available to the public by the Arizona Judicial Branch, in partnership with the Arizona Criminal Justice Commission.

An Order of Protection is a court order that is issued to stop a person from committing domestic violence or from contacting other people protected by the order. The portal will also help you figure out whether you (the plaintiff) and the person from whom you are seeking protection (the defendant) have a qualifying relationship for an Order of Protection.

Contact Information

Web Address
https://azpoint.azcourts.gov/

____

Suicide Prevention

We can all help prevent suicide. The Lifeline provides 24/7, free and confidential support for people in distress, prevention and crisis resources for you or your loved ones, and best practices for professionals. Native Americans, Attempt Survivors, Vetarans, Deaf, Hard of Hearing, Youth, Loss Survivors, ayuda En Espanol, Disaster Survivors, LGBTQ+. We understand that every struggle is different.

Contact Information

Web Address
https://suicidepreventionlifeline.org/
Face Book URL
https://www.facebook.com/800273talk/
Telephone # 1-800-273-8255

Verde Valley Medical Center

269 S Candy Ln, Cottonwood, AZ 86326
At Northern Arizona Healthcare, our Emergency Department care teams can deal with any emergency that comes through the door. Together, we have Level I and Level IV trauma centers that provide around-the-clock coverage in neurosurgery and orthopedic surgery as well as an on-call anesthesiologist.
Our three emergency departments include:
• Flagstaff Medical Center Emergency
• Verde Valley Medical Center Emergency
• Northern Arizona Healthcare- Sedona Emergency

This expertise lets us treat almost any condition or trauma, eliminating the need to travel to Phoenix. With the latest technology and expert, on-call ED physicians and staff, you can trust us to provide you and your loved ones with the best care possible.

Contact Information

Web Address
https://www.nahealth.com/emergency-department
Face Book URL
https://www.facebook.com/NAHVerdeValley/
Telephone # 928-639-6172

____

EMERGENCY

√ Verde Valley Sanctuary

497 Main St. Camp Verde AZ. 86322
Twice Nice Thrift Store with locations in
Cottonwood, Sedona and Camp Verde.
The Verde Valley Sanctuary began in 1993 as
a grassroots organization of women who were
concerned about domestic violence in our
community. The original group of volunteers
began taking crisis calls in their homes and
transporting victims of abuse to the nearest
shelters in Flagstaff, Prescott, and Phoenix. Since
then the Verde Valley Sanctuary has strategically
expanded and now offers comprehensive services
for victims of family violence and assault
including a 28 bed shelter, 24-hour crisis hotline,
advocacy and counseling services, legal support
and community wide education and prevention
programs.
Thrift Store Hours: Tues -Sat 10-5pm

Contact Information

Web Address
https://verdevalleysanctuary.org/shopping/
Face Book URL
https://www.facebook.com/VerdeValleySanctuary
Email: development@verdevalleysanctuary.org
Telephone # 24 Hour Hotline: 800-930-7233
Main Office: 928-634-2511
Fax: 928-649-0769

Yavapai Apache Police Department

2400 West Datsi Ave. Camp Verde, AZ 86322
The Public Safety Program is located in the
Middle Verde tribal community next to the Social
Service building. Public Safety is comprised of
three divisions: police, criminal investigations
and fire/emergency services. The Public Safety
Program provides all public and community safety
measures to all tribal communities. The Yavapai-
Apache Nation is located in the Verde Valley
of Arizona and is comprised of five (5) tribal
communities: Tunlii, Middle Verde, Rimrock,
Camp Verde.

Contact Information

Web Address
https://yavapai-apache.org/directory/yavapai-
apache-police-department/#
Telephone # 928-649-7142 or always dial 911

Yavapai County Jail

3830 N. Commonwealth Drive, Camp Verde, AZ
86322
For a small fee, EMessaging will allow family and
friends to initiate email style messages with up to
six attachments to their loved ones incarcerated
within the Yavapai County Detention Center.
PH 928-567-7734

Contact Information

Web Address
https://www.ycsoaz.gov/inmate-search-and-jail-
information
Telephone # 928-567-7734

Reserved add space for Chamber adds.

Call to reserve space. Must be a member.

1/4 Page $100, 1/2 Page $200, Full Page $400

Reserved add space for Chamber adds.

Call to reserve space. Must be a member.

1/4 Page $100, 1/2 Page $200, Full Page $400

Reserved add space for Chamber adds.

Call to reserve space. Must be a member.

1/4 Page $100, 1/2 Page $200, Full Page $400

NEW TO CAMP VERDE-WATER/POWER

Yavapai County Sheriff's Department

Main Line PHONE: 928-771-3260
Eastern Command - Camp Verde
2830 N. Commonwealth Drive Suite 104
Camp Verde, AZ 86322
The Yavapai County Sheriff's Office mission is to enhance the quality of life in the county by working cooperatively with the public to prevent crime, enforce the law, preserve the peace, and provide a safe environment through professional education programs aimed at promoting community involvement in various community services and crime prevention education. See website for information on: Jail and inmates, media, animal control, forms, community relations, emergency notification system.

Contact Information
Web Address
https://www.ycsoaz.gov/
Face Book URL
https://www.facebook.com/YavapaiCountySheriff
Email: web.sheriff@yavapai.us
Telephone # 928-567-7710

———————————

→New to Camp Verde

WATER & POWER

Arizona Public Service (APS)

120 N. Marina Street, Prescott, Az 86301
Looking for ways to save on your energy bill? We can help you find bill assistance, rebates, tips and tools that work for you.

- Pay your bill
  Start, stop or move service
  Report an outage
  COVID-19 resources

Hours: Mon-Thurs 9AM-1PM
928-776-3636
Contact Information
Web Address
https://www.aps.com/en/residential/home
Face Book URL
https://www.facebook.com/apsfyi
Telephone # 24 hours 602-371-7171
Toll Free 800-253-9405.

———————————

Camp Verde Water System

49 S. 6th Street, Camp Verde, AZ 86322
Call the office for information on water connection and billing.
Hours: Monday-Friday, 8-12, 1-4
Contact Information-
Telephone # 928-567-5281

———————————

NEW TO CAMP VERDE-TRASH/RECYCLE

Unisource Energy Services

UES provides natural gas service in Santa Cruz, Mohave, Yavapai, Coconino and Navajo counties. Account, renewable energy, energy efficiency, community.

*Please report all outages or emergencies to: Emergency Hotline - 1-877-837-4968

Contact Information

Web Address
https://www.uesaz.com/

Face Book URL
https://www.facebook.com/
UniSourceEnergyServices/

Email: uescustomercare@uesaz.com

Telephone # Mon- Fri 7 a.m. - 6 p.m.
1-877-837-4968

Verde Lakes Water

2867 Verde Lakes Dr. #B, Camp Verde, AZ 86322
Verde Lake Water Corporation is dedicated to serving the community of Verde Lake with a steady supply of high quality water.
Hours: Mon, Wed, Fri, 9AM-4PM

Contact Information

Web Address
http://verdelakeswater.com/

Telephone # 928-567-4338

TRASH DISPOSAL & SEWER

Camp Verde Transfer Station

2600 East AZ-260, Camp Verde, Az 86322
The Solid Waste Division is under the Public Works Department. In compliance with all federal and state regulations, the Solid Waste Division is responsible for the operation of 8 waste transfer stations, 2 tire yards, trash patrol in the county right of way, adopt-a-road program, community cleanups, free slash, and post-closure county landfills.

Camp Verde Transfer Station – Green Waste
Until further notice, the Camp Verde Transfer Station will not be accepting green waste.
Hours: Tuesday-Saturday, 8AM- 4PM

Contact Information

Web Address
https://yavapaiaz.gov/publicworks/solid-waste-division

Face Book URL
https://www.facebook.com/pages/Yavapai-County-Public-Works/1006678482708516

Email: web.public.works@yavapaiaz.gov

Telephone # 928-713-8910

Patriot Disposal

9434 East Valley Rd. Prescott, Az 86314
 Our residential garbage service makes waste removal convenient for you. From special pickups to scheduled weekly trash collection, our courteous drivers can be counted on to pick up your household waste on time. Hours: Monday-Friday, 8AM- 4PM

Contact Information

Web Address
http://www.patriotdisposal.com/

Face Book URL
https://www.facebook.com/patriotdisposal

Email: patriot.disposal@yahoo.com

Telephone # 928-775-9000

Guide to Recycling

Your guide to recycling in Camp Verde and the Verde Valley.

Curbside Pick-up

Taylor Waste lets you add a recycling bin to your trash pick-up for about the price of a fancy cappuccino. Recycling gets picked up twice per month. The recycling container is less than half the price of an additional trash can. Taylor Waste does not accept glass. taylorwaste.com/ or 9286492662 Waste Management recycles paper, cardboard, plastic, glass, and tin, aluminum, and steel cans. They also harness methane from their landfills to power homes in Arizona. Click here to view their Sustainability Report. www.wm.com or 800-796-9696

Materials should be clean and dry when recycling. Patriot Disposal gathers the trash and recycling in one bin and removes many recyclable materials directly from the trash at the Freedom Recycling Center. They process 100% of the residential material they pick up. Just put everything in one bin and they take care of the rest—and it's included in your trash removal service. www. patriotdisposal.com or 928-203-9995

Business Recycling

Contact Sedona Recycles for commercial recycling pick-up at 928-204-1185. Drop-Off, Mail-In, or Schedule a Pick-up. The Cottonwood Transfer Station allows free recycling drop-off. They are located at 1500 West Mingus Avenue in Cottonwood and open 7:30 a.m.-3:30 p.m., Tuesday-Saturday. They do not accept appliances containing freon. Recycling drop-off locations that are still available until further notice include Mingus Union High School in Cottonwood (1801 East Fir Street) and behind the Rimrock Post Office (5235 North Lookout Point Road).

APS will pick up your refrigerator and pay you $30. Call 877-514-6654 for more information. Camp Verde Transfer Station: Drop-off used motor oil for no charge at 2600 E. Highway 260, open 8:00 a.m.-4:00 p.m., Tuesday-Saturday.

Verde Valley Habitat for Humanity: you can drop-off donations or have large donatable items picked up (like furniture, appliances, and construction material). Drop-off at Verde Valley Habitat for Humanity, 737 S. Main Street in Cottonwood. Call 928-649-6788 before dropping off items or to schedule a time for them to pick items up directly from you! And your donation is tax-deductible. Habitat for Humanity does not accept mattresses.

Sedona Recycles: drop-off items to be recycled at 2280 Shelby Drive in Sedona. They recycle a slew of materials, including electronics, batteries, printer cartridges, packing materials, paper, glass, and even Styrofoam blocks. Sedona Recycles does not accept Cathode Ray Tube (CRT) monitors and televisions, plastic bags, plate glass, ceramic, mirrors, waxed cardboard, and some other items. For a list of accepted materials, fees, and a reuse and disposal guide, visit www.sedonarecycles.org/

You can recycle CFL bulbs, rechargeable batteries, and cell phones at Home Depot, plastic bags at Bashas, and desktop printer ink cartridges at Office Max.
Costco offers a large-scale mail-in recycling program for inkjet and laser toner cartridges. Visit www.costco.com/ink-toner-recycle.html for more information.

Click here for a list of locations to dispose of hazardous chemicals and other household waste. Or contact the Yavapai County Solid Waste department at 928-771-3183 more information on disposing hazardous household waste.

Free Transfer Station Dump Days/Slash Drop-Off

NEW TO CAMP VERDE-TRASH/RECYCLE

Free Community Clean Up days in Camp Verde are typically for about nine days at the end of March and beginning of April (usually Thursdays through Sundays). During this time, most drop-offs at the Camp Verde Transfer Station are free. Dates vary for other Transfer Stations in Yavapai County.

The annual free slash drop-off program is available at Yavapai County transfer stations for two months April 1-June 1, 2018 during normal operating hours. Get rid of brush, branches, grass, leaves, and yard trimmings.

For Transfer Station locations, fees, hours, and for the free dump/slash calendar, please visit www.yavapai.us/publicworks/solid-waste-division Other times of the year, slash drop-off at the Camp Verde Transfer Station is only $5 per truckload and $10-$15 per trailer. You can usually even pick up free mulch while you're there!

Contact Information

Web Address
https://heartofcampverde.com/camp-verde-recycling-guide/

Taylor Waste

319 S 6th Street,   Cottonwood, Az 86326
Residential trash, garbage, and waste collection and recycling services. Locally Owned and Operated. Offering residential garbage collection along with curb side recycling in Prescott Valley, Dewey, Humboldt, Mayer, Sedona, Camp Verde, Cottonwood, Rimrock, Cornville, Lake Montezuma and the Entire Verde Valley.
Hours: Mon-Fri, 8AM- 5PM
Contact Information
Web Address
https://www.taylorwaste.com/
Face Book URL
https://www.facebook.com/taylorwastetrash?_rdr
Telephone # 928-649-2662

Town of Camp Verde Waste Water Division

395 South Main St. Camp Verde, AZ
Moved the Payment Drop in front of Camp Verde Parks and Recreation Office. Sewer.
Contact Information
Web Address
http://www.campverde.az.gov
Telephone # 928-567-6794

Waste Management Yavapai

23355 East Hwy 169   Dewey, Az 86327
Residential Waste and Recycling.
We offer reliable trash and recycling pickup services for the waste everyday life creates. Free Setup and Delivery. We will setup your account and deliver your containers for free. Up to $75 in value. No annual contract required. Residential waste & recycling services are available without an annual contract. Drivers Trained For Safety. We have an industry-leading focus on driver training and safety. Business Waste and Recycling, Roll off Dumpster Rental, Business Waste Compactors, Special waste streams, national accounts. Hours:

NEW TO CAMP VERDE-INTERNET

Mon-Fri, 7AM- 4PM Sat-Sun, 8AM-12PM

Contact Information
Web Address
https://www.wm.com/
Face Book URL
https://www.facebook.com/WasteManagement/
Telephone # 928-779-6050

PHONE, INTERNET

CenturyLink

109 E Arnold St, Camp Verde, AZ 86322
In Camp Verde, one of the most well known Internet service providers is CenturyLink. CenturyLink brings both DSL and fiber optic coverage to this city, making it easy for each consumer to decide which plan and speed range fits their needs. Coverage is accessible in all of Camp Verde and many other nearby Arizona towns and villages.
Contact Information
Web Address
http://www.internetservicecampverde.com/
Telephone # 928-852-4572

Hughes Net- Satellite

HughesNet makes getting satellite Internet simple. Our online experts will happily answer your questions and help you select a plan that is right for you and your family. . Get connected to HughesNet today in your Camp Verde home and get the credibility you deserve. Call 1-877-481-8912 now to get Internet service in Camp Verde!
Contact Information
Web Address
https://www.hughesnetplans.com/satellite-internet/Arizona/C/Camp-Verde/
Telephone # 1-877-481-8912

Sparklight (Formerly Cable One)

235 S. 6th Street   Cottonwood, Az 86326
Hours: Monday-Tuesday-Thursday, 9AM-12:30PM, Wednesday-Friday 1PM-5PM
Contact Information
Web Address
https://www.sparklight.com/
Face Book URL
https://www.facebook.com/SparklightCares/
Telephone # (877) 692-2253

SuddenLink-Cable

All plans Include: Speeds up to 940 Mbps, Flexible packages available, Installation and equipment fees may apply.
Contact Information
Web Address
https://decisiondata.org/tv-internet-by-zip/86322-internet/#suddenlink
Telephone # 833-303-7677

NEW TO CAMP VERDE-SATELLITE

Viasat-Satellite

If you are new to the Camp Verde AZ area, or if you are a longtime resident looking for unlimited rural internet, Viasat Satellite Internet (formerly Exede) has great options to bring broadband wireless internet to your home or business. Viasat wireless broadband internet plans deliver download speeds up to 100 Mbps with unlimited data. Your address will determine which Viasat internet plan is available to you. If you currently have an internet service provider, call us today to compare our unlimited high-speed rural satellite internet with the internet plan you have. When you choose Viasat as your rural satellite internet service provider, we take care of all the details for you in Camp Verde. All you do is schedule an installation time, and a Viasat technician will come to your home or business to install your satellite dish and set up your broadband wireless internet router. If you need help with getting your computer or wireless devices connected to the internet, the technician will be happy to oblige.

Contact Information

Web Address

http://www.rsinc.com/internet/arizona/c/camp-verde/

Telephone # 877-697-2926

SATELLITE

Direct TV

Tuesday-Saturday, 5AM-10PM

Contact Information

Web Address

https://www.directvonline.com

Telephone # 855-909-9319

Dish TV

Tuesday-Saturday, 8AM-6PM

Contact Information

Web Address

https://www.dish.com

Telephone # 480-788-3169

PROPANE

Amerigas - Flame

624 N Industrial Dr. Camp Verde, AZ 86322

Hours: Monday-Friday, 8AM-4PM

Contact Information

Web Address

https://www.amerigas.com/

Telephone # 928-567-4099

Ferrellgas

523 N Industrial Dr. Camp Verde, AZ 86322

Camp Verde, Az 86322

Hours: Monday-Friday, 8Am-10:30A. 11:30A- 5P

Contact Information

Web Address

https://www.ferrellgas.com/

Telephone # 928-567-3274

NEW TO CAMP VERDE-PROPANE

Graves Propane
3591 Old Hwy 279, Camp Verde, Az 86322
Hours: Monday-Friday, 8AM-5PM
Contact Information
Web Address
https://www.johngravespropane.com
Telephone # (928) 567-2425

PROPANE REFILL

Camp Verde Feed & Country Store
584 S. Main Street, Camp Verde, Az 86322
Camp Verde Feeds & Country Store, in Camp Verde, AZ, is your local go-to for hunting & fishing supplies, licenses & equipment, bait, ammo, pet feed & supplies, horse shoes, electric fencing, tack and more! Have a drive-in window. Can pick up ammo and local steaks through the window. Will refill propane. Check in at the office and drive around to the back. Hours Monday-Saturday, 6A-8P Sunday, 7A-8P
Contact Information
Web Address
http://campverdefeedstore.com/
Face Book URL
https://www.facebook.com/CVFeedstore/
Email: campverdefeedstore@gmail.com
Telephone # 928-567-3351

Circle K
24 W. Finnie Flat Rd. Camp Verde, Az 86322
Brand New built building with extensive beverage bar and snacks. Excellent lighting. Safe stop any time of the day. Fresh coffee.
Hours: open 24 hours.
Contact Information
Web Address
https://www.circlek.com
Telephone # 928-567-4067

Good 2 Go in Chevron Station
1897 Pueblo Ridge Rd. Camp Verde, Az 86322
Good 2 Go Stores provides a family-friendly destination for travelers to refuel and restock on snacks, beverages, and propane.
Hours: Monday-Sunday, 5AM-Midnight
Contact Information
Web Address
https://www.good2gostores.com
Telephone # 928-567-1463

Minute Mart #48 In Shell Station
1673 W, State Route 260, Camp Verde, Az 86322
For travelers to refuel and restock on snacks, beverages, and propane. Hours: Open 24 Hours
Contact Information
Telephone # 928-567-3886

AUTO REPAIR

BG Automotive Services
673 S. 1st #2, Camp Verde, Az 86322
Monday-Friday, 8AM-5PM
Contact Information
Telephone # 928-567-9280

NEW TO CAMP VERDE-AUTOMOTIVE

Camp Verde Automotive LLC

27 W. General Crook Tr. Camp Verde, Az 86322
Repair services, preventative maintenance, appointment request, warranty. Welcome to the CAMP VERDE AUTOMOTIVE LLC website! We hope you will enjoy browsing through our website, and that you will find a lot of useful information here. We pay great attention to the quality of our products and services. You can find detailed information about our products and services online or contact our customer service team for help. Monday-Friday, 7:30AM-5PM

Contact Information

Web Address
http://campverdeautomotivellc.com/
Telephone # 928-567-3431

Kaizen Collision Center

1900 N. Moonrise Dr. Camp Verde, Az 86322
Glass repair, collision repair.
Monday-Friday, 8AM-5PM

Contact Information

Web Address
https://www.kaizenautocare.com/body-shop-camp-verde-az/
Face Book URL
https://www.facebook.com/KaizenCollisi on/?eid=ARAaxPXiI6ys3-5Q7s2Ti2U7_ CiGkRUyrNPjDC0P2USa919kEsIu-qrTBo4CxDt0bkEcoB0iinKJ4owd
Email: support@kaizenautocare.com
Telephone # 928-567-7270

Pete Clark Auto Repair LLC

712 Monte Verde Ln. Camp Verde, AZ 86322
Monday-Friday, 9AM-5PM

Contact Information

Telephone # 928-254-1819

TirePro

671 Finnie Flat Rd. Camp Verde, AZ 86322
If you are looking for automotive service done right, you want Tire Pro Automotive. From preventive maintenance to brake repair, Tire Pro Automotive has got you covered! Stop by today if you are near Camp Verde, AZ, Lake Montezuma, AZ, Village of Oak Creek, AZ, and surrounding areas. We offer tires for sale, mobile tire service, fleet service. Monday-Friday, 7:30AM-5PM, Saturday, 8AM-12PM

Contact Information

Web Address
https://www.tireproautomotive.com/
Face Book URL
https://www.facebook.com/tireproautomotive/
Email: cherie@tireproautomotive.com
Telephone # 928-567-6338

NEW TO CAMP VERDE-AUTOMOTIVE

AUTO PARTS

AutoZone
992 Finnie Flat Rd, Camp Verde, AZ 86322
Monday-Saturday, 7:30AM-9PM, Sunday, 8AM-8PM
Contact Information
Web Address
https://www.autozone.com/locations/az/camp-verde/992-west-finnie-flat-rd.html
Telephone # 928-325-6145

____

Napa Auto Parts-Camp Verde
522 Finnie Flat Rd. Camp Verde, Az 86322
Monday-Friday, 7:30AM-5:30PM, Saturday, 7:30AM-3PM
Contact Information
Web Address
https://www.napaonline.com/
Telephone # 928-567-3356

____

O'Reilly Auto Parts
1016 W Finnie Flat Rd. Camp Verde, Az 86322
Mon-Sat, 7:30AM-9PM, Sunday, 8AM-8PM
Contact Information
Web Address
https://www.oreillyauto.com/
Telephone # 928-202-3627

____

Verde Valley Glass-Auto
873 Howard Rd. #7, Camp Verde, Az 86322
Locally owned and operated auto glass shop with 12 years of auto glass installation experience. We work with all insurance companies and offer the best cash prices in the Verde Valley, AZ! We are licensed and insured, and we offer a customer satisfaction guarantee along with a lifetime workmanship warranty. We use the highest quality materials, glass and the newest tools in the industry. We are Sika certified and rust prevention certified. We also service Sedona, AZ. We come to your home or office. Next day service is available and we offer free mobile service for Camp Verde, Cottonwood, and Sedona areas. Cars & Trucks we work on: Luxury,Exotics, Domestic, Foreign.
Monday-Friday, 8AM-5PM
Contact Information
Web Address
https://vvautoglass.com/
Face Book URL
https://www.facebook.com/howell2988/
Email: verdevalleyautoglass@yahoo.com
Telephone # 928-963-4321

____

LAUNDROMAT

Fort Verde Laundromat

348 S. Main Street
Camp Verde, Az 86322
Open 24 Hours self-service laundromat.
Contact Information
Telephone # 928-821-0670

____

Mamaw's Laundry

1675 E. Cottonwood St. Suite G
Cottonwood, Az 86326
Self-service laundromat. New and improved
folding and lounge area. 4 sizes of washers. Heavy
duty washers. Personal wash, fold and ironing.
Free WiFi.
Hours: Sunday-Thursday 6AM-9PM Friday-
Saturday 6AM-8PM (Hours might differ)
Contact Information
Web Address
https://mamaws-laundry.business.site/
Telephone # 970-430-0181

____

The Laundry Room

2593 S. Union Dr. Cottonwood, Az 86326
A Verde Village Community Laundromat Open 24
hours, 7 days a week, 365 days a year
The Laundry Room is a uniquely local owned
and operated community Laundromat with well
maintained Speed Queen equipment, including:
(22) Top Load washing machines $2.00/load
(2) 40 pound washer extractors (3 load) $4.00/load
(13) 45 pound Gas Dryers $.25/8 minutes
Located in a quiet, safe community.
Unattended with 24 hour surveillance cameras.
Operations Manager maintains laundromat &
machines daily.
Open 24 Hours
Contact Information
Face Book URL
https://www.facebook.com/
TheLaundryRoomCottonwood/
Telephone # 928-282-5028

____

DRY CLEANING

Spot Masters

718 S Main St. Cottonwood, Az 86322
Hours: Monday-Friday, 7AM-6PM Saturday
9AM-3PM Sunday - Closed (Hours might differ)
Contact Information
Telephone # 928-634-0044

____

TRANSPORTATION

Ace Xpress Shuttle Service

298 S. 6th Street, Cottonwood, Az 86326
 Travel slots remain available 7 days a week from 4AM-11PM. Office: Monday-Friday 9am-6pm, Saturday- 12pm-5pm, Sunday- Closed. Messages left outside of these hours will be answered the next business day. Phoenix-Sky Harbor

Serving Northern Arizona with daily door-to-door shuttle service Cottonwood and Sedona to Phoenix Sky Harbor Airport.

*   Cottonwood
    Camp Verde
    Clarkdale
    Cornville
    Lake Montezuma
    Rimrock
    Sedona
    Verde Santa Fe
    Village of Oak Creek
    Retreats: Angel Valley, Grace Grove,
    Sanctuary
    Schools: Sedona Sky Academy, Southwestern
    Academy

Contact Information
Web Address
https://www.acexshuttle.com/
Telephone # 928-649-2720

____

Enterprise Rent-A-Car

483 S Main St, Cottonwood, AZ 86326
car rental, exotic cars, one way rentals, one way rental.
Contact Information
Web Address
https://www.enterprise.com/en/car-rental/
locations/us/az/cottonwood-50b2.html
Telephone # 928-634-0049

Groome Transportation

Groome Transportation Airport Shuttle Service provides safe, reliable, and convenient intercity airport transportation connecting regional cities to major hub airports. With shared shuttle services between over 100 cities and 13 airports in the US, getting to and from the airport has never been easier.
Take the stress out of travel & let us do the driving. Groome stops at Chevron which is at Wendy's off of I 17. Runs hourly. People park out front of Wendy's when they catch the shuttle. They take you right to the flight terminal. Can book easily from your phone and they keep track of you and your flight helping if your plane runs late.
Contact Information
Web Address
https://groometransportation.com/
Telephone # 928-350-8466

____

NEW TO CAMP VERDE-LICENSEES

Jones Ford Verde Valley Rental Cars

E Coury Dr, Cottonwood, AZ 86322

If you just want to rent a car, SUV or Minivan and not read all the information below click here to book your rental. Call and speak with our Rental Manager. (928) 782-8923 Maybe your car is getting fixed up by our expert team and you just need a rental for the day to shop here in Camp Verde, or maybe you just need a ride to or from the airport. Whatever the reason is we have exactly what you are looking for at a price that will make sense for your needs. Questions and Answers about Car Rental in Camp Verde.

What Do I Need to Rent a Vehicle?

A Valid Driver's License.

Proof of Insurance

Be 25 Years of Age or Older

Contact Information

Web Address

https://www.jonesfordverdevalley.com/

Email: tim@jonesfordverde.com.

Telephone # 928-782-8923

____

LICENSES

ADOT & DMV Offices

525 S.12th Street, Cottonwood, Az 86322

Licenses.

Monday-Friday, 8AM-5PM

Contact Information

Web Address

https://azdot.gov

Face Book URL

https://www.facebook.com/AZDOT/

Telephone # Please call 602-712-2700 for assistance. Toll Free 800-251-5866

____

Footwork Auto License and Title

656 S. Main Street, Cottonwood, Az 86326

FooteWork provides complete full service vehicle registration and title services and issues Driver Licenses. Registration information, MVD forms and procedures for registering and titling a vehicle in Cottonwood, Arizona. Licensed and bonded, FooteWork processes your title work while you wait. For a nominal convenience fee, you'll leave our office with a new title, registration or license plate in as little as 10 minutes!

Hours: Monday-Friday, 8A-5P, Saturday 9A-12P

Contact Information

Web Address

https://footework.com/

Face Book URL

https://www.facebook.com/FooteWorkPrescott/

Email: info@footework.com

Telephone # Prescott 928-771-9015 | Prescott Valley 928-759-8575 | Cottonwood 928-649-9247 Williams 928-635-2006

____

Town of Camp Verde-Business License

473 South Main Street, Suite 102, Camp Verde, Arizona 86322

Contact Information

Web Address

https://www.campverde.az.gov/business/business-licenses-2/

Telephone # 928-554-0000

____

SCHOOLS

American Heritage Academy
132 W. General Crook Tr. Camp Verde, Az 86322
Contact Information
Web Address
https://ahacottonwood.org/
Face Book URL
https://www.facebook.com/pages/American%20
Heritage%20Academy/317615035113472/
Telephone # 928-567-0462

____

Camp Verde Elementary School
200 Camp Lincoln Rd.Camp Verde, Az 86322
Providing students a safe and caring environment
in which knowledge, skills, and attitudes enable
learners to become productive citizens.
Contact Information
Web Address
https://campverdeelementaryschool.com/
Face Book URL
https://www.facebook.com/
campverdeelementaryschool/
Telephone # 928-567-8060

____

Camp Verde High School
1326 S Montezuma Castle Hwy
Camp Verde, Az 86322
Respect, Integrity, Positive Relationships,
Accountability. Providing students a safe and
caring environment in which knowledge, skills,
and attitudes enable learners to become productive
citizens
Contact Information
Web Address
http://campverdehighschool.com/
Face Book URL
https://www.facebook.com/pages/Camp%20
Verde%20High%20School/122379157832228/
Email: cvcbacampverde@gmail.com
Telephone # 928-567-8035

Camp Verde Middle School
370 Camp Lincoln Rd.
Camp Verde, Az 86322
Contact Information
Web Address
https://www.campverdeschools.net/#
Face Book URL
https://www.facebook.com/pages/Camp%20
Verde%20Middle%20School/729215313833545/
Telephone # 928-567-8000

____

Camp Verde School District
410 Camp Lincoln Rd. Camp Verde, Az 86322
Contact Information
Web Address
https://www.campverdeschools.net/
Face Book URL
https://www.facebook.com/Camp-Verde-Unified-
School-District-165368003616051/
Telephone # 928-567-3382

____

Ed Options High School
155 S Montezuma Castle Hwy. Camp Verde, Az
86322
EdOptions High School Learning Center and
EdOptions Preparatory Academy are free,
independent public high schools in Phoenix and
throughout Arizona that provide each student
with the access, opportunity, and support needed
to earn their high school diploma. EdOptions
High School is dedicated to providing students
with award-winning curriculum that aligns to
state standards, scheduling flexibility, and an
educational environment of high expectations
and individual success. We merge technology and
content delivery with highly qualified classroom
and online teachers to provide each student with
superior opportunities for academic success.
Contact Information
Web Address
https://eohighschool.com/
Telephone # 928-433-0333

√ Osher Life Long Learning Institute

Classes designed to help the brain stay active.
Non-profit offering classes on and off campuses as
well as ZOOM.

Contact Information

Web Address
https://www.yc.edu/v6/olli-sedona-
verde/?locale=en
Telephone # 928-649-4275

Sedona Center of Yavapai College
4215 Arts Village Dr
Sedona, AZ 86336
Telephone # 928-649-4275

South Verde High School

Camp Verde ON-Line High
462 S. Main Street. Camp Verde, Az 86322
The Camp Verde Online High School is an
Accredited High School. It is an Arizona State
Board approved AOI (Arizona Online School).
This online instruction system expands learning
opportunities for students throughout the state.

Contact Information

Web Address
http://southverdehighschool.campverdeschools.
net/
Face Book URL
https://www.facebook.com/South-Verde-High-
School-908972655790073
Telephone # 928-567-8076

United Christian School

903 Finnie Flat Rd. Camp Verde, Az 86322

Contact Information

Web Address
https://www.cvucs.org/
Face Book URL
https://www.facebook.com/United-Christian-
School-Camp-Verde-2078496025778931
Telephone # 928-567-0415

Yavapai College SBDC

601 W Black Hills Dr
Clarkdale, AZ 86324
Telephone # 928-649-5550

REALTORS

Arizona Central Land & Home

348 S. Main Street #5, Camp Verde, Az 86322
Gary and Susi Thompson REALTORS®
Welcome to Arizona Central Land and Home
REAL ESTATE SALES web site. We are here to
work for you. Customer Satisfaction is our Top
Priority. Serving: Camp Verde, Rimrock, Lake
Montezuma, Cottonwood, Cornville, and Sedona
Arizona
Hours: Monday-Friday, 9AM-5PM

Contact Information

Web Address
https://www.outstandingagents.com/
Face Book URL
https://www.facebook.com/ArizonaCentral
Email: gary@outstandingagents.com
Telephone # 928-567-2770

Beth & James Adams Real Estate Agency

2130 S Squaw Peak Rd. Camp Verde, Az 86322

Contact Information

Web Address
https://www.adamshomesaz.com/
Face Book URL
https://www.facebook.com/goadamsteam
Telephone # 928-362-0658

Reserved add space for Chamber adds.

Call to reserve space. Must be a member.

1/4 Page $100, 1/2 Page $200, Full Page $400

Reserved add space for Chamber adds.

Call to reserve space. Must be a member.

1/4 Page $100, 1/2 Page $200, Full Page $400

Reserved add space for Chamber adds.

Call to reserve space. Must be a member.

1/4 Page $100, 1/2 Page $200, Full Page $400

NEW TO CAMP VERDE-Realtors

Camp Verde Realty Inc.

295 S. Main Street, Camp Verde, AZ 86322
Hours: Monday-Friday, 9AM-5PM, Saturday,
9AM-3PM
Web Address
https://www.campverderealty.com/
Telephone # 9285676474

Barbara Parsons Sales Associate
"I have lived in the Verde Valley since 1997 and
have been a licensed realtor since 1999. The valley
is in a high-desert area, surrounded by beautiful
mountains in the approximate center of the state.
Email: Parsonsfamily4@msn.com

Telephone # 928-821-0955 Cell Phone

Bridgett Bowers Sales Associate/Property
Management
I have been working for Camp Verde Realty since
2005. I am hard-working and dedicated and I love
living in Camp Verde!

Telephone # 928-300-2533 Cell Phone

Dianna Stevens Sales Associate
I have been a Realtor for about 15 years. There are
so many wonderful areas to choose from.
Email: dianna_stevens@msn.com

Telephone # 928-607-7677 Cell Phone

Bill Carter Designated Broker
Sedona Verde Valley Association of Realtors
Telephone # 928-567-6474

Rob Witt, Arizona Prime Real Estate

400 Finnie Flat Rd. Camp Verde, Az 86322
Rob Witt Arizona Prime Real Estate. Clients
needs have been my number one priority for 34
years and running. Trust is earned not granted and
earning trust for me is all about protecting clients
real estate investments. I consider real estate
investments to be a home, which in many cases is
the single largest investment in a client's portfolio,
and commercial real estate.
Hours: Monday-Saturday, 8AM-8PM
Telephone # 928-451-6881
Contact Information
Web Address
https://www.realtor.com/realestateagents/robert-
witt_sedona_az_665266_822789358
Telephone # 928-451-6881

United Country Real Estate, Verde Valley Property

564 S Main Street
Camp Verde, Az 86322
Contact Information
Telephone # 928-718-2020

Community Resources

√ Abide Maternity Home
Hope Women's Center.

A place for pregnant women and mothers who need more support than they are currently receiving. Our goal is to equip women with the skills and resources needed to move forward in a life filled with newfound hope.

- Housing for pregnant and parenting women
  Weekly personal coaching for men and women
  New Life Thrift Shop
  Free Pregnancy Testing

Contact Information

Web Address
https://hopewomenscenter.org/
Face Book URL
 https://www.facebook.com/abidematernityhome
Telephone # 928-567-5433

———————

Arizona Crisis Team

Arizona Crisis Team. (ACT) is a non-profit organization that provides emotional, practical, and resource assistance to citizens who have been impacted by any type of crisis - 24 hours a day, 365 days a year.

Contact Information

Web Address
https://www.azcrisisteam.org/Control-Panel/Home
Telephone # 928-713-6625

———————

AZ Court Help

The website, administered by the Arizona Bar Foundation through the support of the Arizona Supreme Court, is in partnership with the courts across Arizona and their Law Libraries. Coconino County Court assisted in spearheading the development of the website in conjunction with their Virtual Resource Center, Legal Talks, assisted by the Attorney General's Office, the State Library of Arizona, and Department of Economic Security.

Contact Information

Web Address
https://azcourthelp.org/

———————

Beaver Creek Adult Center

The Beaver Creek Adult Center is a 501(c)(3) non-profit corporation and all operations are done by volunteers. We don't get mail at 4250 Zuni Way. We have a P.O. Box 433 in Rimrock.
Resource Fairs at the Adult Center. We have people available to provide information and help about resources available in the community. Call Bonnie at 510-761-0439 if you have questions.

Contact Information

Web Address
https://beavercreekadultcenter.com/
Face Book URL
https://www.facebook.com/1bcac
Email: bcac4556@gmail.com
Telephone # 928-567-4556

———————

Bread of Life Food Sharing

Offering free food boxes distributed at 1575 Sullivan Lane Camp Verde Arizona.
Call for emergency food boxes.

Contact Information

Web Address
https://www.breadoflifeaz.org/
Telephone # 928-567-6931

COMMUNITY RESOURCES

Camp Verde Arena Association

A non - profit organization building an educational economic viable multi-use equine facility for the greater Camp Verde community. Anything Rodeo!

Contact Information

Web Address
http://www.campverdearena.com/
Face Book URL
https://www.facebook.com/campverdearenaassoc
Email: campverdearena@gmail.com
Telephone # 928-821-0476

____

Camp Verde AZ Neighbors and Friends Facebook Site

3.5 K members
Welcome to the group Camp Verde AZ Neighbors and Friends. Here you will find Camp Verde community information, events, news, and nostalgia. You have known us, followed us, and been our friends at (simply) Camp Verde. Creating this group allows us to better describe who we are and what we do for our community, as well as encourage your participation.
We are not affiliated with the 'government' of Camp Verde (ie: Town of Camp Verde), although we follow their websites and their official Facebook Visitor page for up-to-date information to share here.
We hope you enjoy being a member of this group, and participating in discussions, spreading the word, and sharing pertinent Camp Verde AZ information.

Contact Information

Face Book URL
https://www.facebook.com/
groups/1764222540514814
Email: cvcbacampverde@gmail.com
Telephone # 928-203-6863

Camp Verde Buy Nothing Facebook Site

This group was created to get rid of unwanted items that are collecting dust. Instead of throwing them away post a picture and gift it to someone who can use it. The larger the group, the closer to the community we become.

Contact Information

Face Book URL
https://www.facebook.com/
groups/2990959127605364

____

Camp Verde Chamber and Business Alliance

CVBA is a dynamic network dedicated to the prosperity of businesses-new and old, small or large--in Camp Verde and throughout the Verde Valley. We honor the rich heritage of our community and enthusiastically support future development. We are committed to providing representation, promotion, and resources for the business community. The cost of membership is $75 per year, beginning on July 1st.

Contact Information

Web Address
https://campverdebiz.com/
Face Book URL
https://www.facebook.com/campverdechamber
Email: cvcbacampverde@gmail.com
Telephone # 928-203-6863

____

COMMUNITY RESOURCES

√ Camp Verde Community Library

130 Black Bridge Road, Camp Verde, AZ 86322
The library offers several community services including:

- Literacy Program (GED)
- Tech help
- Tax aid services
- Help with medical insurance
- Children's reading hour.
- Rooms for use free of charge
- Books, books, books
- Friends of the Library office
- Visit their web page to find out more!

Contact Information
Web Address
https://www.campverde.az.gov/departments/
community-library
Face Book URL
https://www.facebook.com/campverdelibrary
Email: library@campverde.az.gov
Telephone # 928-554-8380

Library Technical Help

Are you having trouble figuring out how to use or update your mobile device? Do you need someone who is patient, knowledgeable, and has an affinity for solving tech issues to help you? Make an appointment or drop in for one-to-one help from Wendy any Wednesday between 9:00a and noon. She can assist you with your tech issues and help you learn how to download and use library apps and resources. Give her a call at PH 928-554-8385.Contact Information
Telephone # 928-554-8385.

Camp Verde Neighborhood Watch Facebook Site

Camp Verde Neighborhood Watch is a group where you may post general questions or info pertaining to Camp Verde or the surrounding areas and or find help or place warnings etc. Great site to keep an eye on the neighborhood. 1.2 K members
Contact Information
Face Book URL
https://www.facebook.com/
groups/600285443438760

Camp Verde Promotions

PO Box 1970 Camp Verde, AZ 86322
We are a non profit to promote festivals in the Camp Verde, Az area.
Contact Information
Face Book URL
https://www.facebook.com/campverdepromotions

COMMUNITY RESOURCES

Camp Verde Senior Center and Thrift Store

The senior center thrift store is open M-F 9A to 3P. Located at 263 Maryvale Drive Camp Verde. Currently, they offer daily, weekday lunches. The food is home-cooked, plentiful and the company is lively. We have Wi-Fi internet services, a pool table, and other offerings. Be sure to visit our thrift store downstairs while you stop by for lunch.

Contact Information

Face Book URL
https://www.facebook.com/The-Camp-Verde-Senior-Center-Thrift-Store-941773319179480
Telephone # 928-567-6356

Camp Verde Unified School District 28 Facebook Site

Providing students a safe and caring environment in which knowledge, skills, and attitudes enable learners to become productive.

Contact Information

Face Book URL
https://www.facebook.com/cvusd28

Camp Verde Youth Football and Cheer Sports League Facebook Site

Youth sports league for football and cheer. Check out their Facebook page for more information. CV Youth Football and Cheer FB

Contact Information

Face Book URL
https://www.facebook.com/
CampVerdeYouthFootball/about/

Catholic Charities

St. Frances Cabrini Catholic Church
781 Cliffs Pkwy, Camp Verde, AZ 86322
Catholic Charities staff and volunteers monitors the needs of central and northern Arizona communities and responds by providing life-changing services that protect and nurture children, help strengthen families and assist individuals in crisis - growing to serve communities. Join us in this incredible work and be a miracle to someone today. Largest distribution of money to help those in need in Camp Verde in 2020.

Veterans and their families
Sex-trafficked survivors
Victims of domestic abuse
Refugees
Homeless
Foster care
Adoption
Pregnancy counseling
North Star Youth Partnership
Westside Head Start early education
Affordable housing

Contact Information

Web Address
https://www.catholiccharitiesaz.org/
Face Book URL
https://www.facebook.com/CatholicCharitiesAZ
Email: info@cc-az.org
Telephone # 928-567-3543

https://campverdebiz.com/   Camp Verde Chamber & Business Alliance

COMMUNITY RESOURCES

Copper Canyon Fire and Medical District

Information on escape routes, communication, notes on drug busts, overdoses in your area. Emergency Management/Response Employment Opportunities
How about a coloring book?
Download or order copies of our advanced Fire Scientist Coloring Book - FREE - at http://ow.ly/VXDs50DUmrq. #coloringbookmonday #coloringbook #color #firescience #prescribedfire FIND Outdoors
Face Book URL
https://www.facebook.com/CopperCanyonFMD

√ Hope Women's Center

77 General Crook Trail
928-567-5433 or 928-713-7007 after hours
Pregnancy option hotline: 8007124357
We do this through a multitude of **FREE**, confidential services and programs which include:

- 1:1 Mentoring and Support Groups
- Parenting classes
- Life Skills and Faith Based Education Classes
- Grief Support and Celebrate Recovery
- Rise Above Abuse and Anger Management
- Classes for birth moms with children in Foster Care or at risk of DCS removal
- Pregnancy Testing and Prenatal Classes
- ROSES Program for Pregnant & moms of Newborns
- Specialized Maternal Mental Health support
- Childcare (0-5) for mothers attending Hope
- Hope Heals - Crisis Counseling & Support
- Hope at Work - Job Skills Classes/ Training
- Maternity Home for pregnant and parenting moms
- Points earned for programs can be used for Material Assistance such as utilities**, transportation, food, clothing, personal care items, household items, and baby/ child products

Contact Information
Web Address

https://hopewomenscenter.org/
Face Book URL
https://www.facebook.com/abidematernityhome
Email: Info@AbideMaternityHome.com
Telephone # 928-567-5433 or 928-713-7007 after hours. Pregnancy option hotline: 1-800-712-4357

Manzanita Outreach Food Sharing

Manzanita Outreach fills the gaps within the Yavapai County food assistance supply chain, sharing food with kindness and dignity. MOhelp.org is a community service program that helps neighbors discover where and when food is shared in their community.
Face Book URL https://www.facebook.com/KAHVV/
Telephone # 928-649-5772

Music in the Stacks

Music in the Stacks is a showcase of local and national musicians who entertain regularly in Northern Arizona. There are 4-6 different performers during the show, with a rotating variety each month.
Many concerts feature the following talented local musicians: Gary Simpkins, Christy Fisher, Mike McReynolds, Tony Cook, and Matt Fabritz.
Camp Verde Community Library is located just off of Montezuma Castle Highway at 130 Black Bridge Road, Camp Verde AZ. For more information about this or any other library program, visit the library's website or call.
Contact Information
Web Address
https://www.campverde.az.gov/departments/community-library
Face Book URL
https://www.facebook.com/campverdelibrary
Email: library@campverde.az.gov
Telephone # 928-554-8380

COMMUNITY RESOURCES

√ NACOG
Northern Arizona Council of Governments EWD

Services include Area on Aging, Head Start, Help with utilities, firewood, propane, Weatherization, economic/workplace development, home program CDBG, regional planning, Route 66 Browfield site revitalization.

Northern Arizona Council of Governments is a nonprofit corporation representing local governments to provide a wide variety of services within Apache, Coconino, Navajo and Yavapai Counties.

Solving common problems. Transcending geographical boundaries. Improving local communities. These are just a few of the tasks of the Northern Arizona Council of Governments (NACOG), a group of local governments representing Apache, Coconino, Navajo and Yavapai Counties. NACOG staff works with local governments to address similar issues faced by the communities within the region.

NACOG's Head Start Division provides comprehensive child development and family support services to economically disadvantaged children and their families.

NACOG's Human & Community Services Division is committed to the development of human and community services in areas ranging from supporting equal opportunities for persons with disabilities and delivering services to older individuals, to combating the conditions of poverty.

NACOG's Economic and Workforce Development Division helps build economic success through workforce development partnerships. Comprehensive economic development planning for workforce, business services and tourism development is a major focus, as well as public works and infrastructure development for sustainable economic growth.

NACOG's Planning Division recognizes that studying area population and demographics is critical to planning a viable transportation system. NACOG provides these services to local governments, along with estimates and projections for population growth. The division also participates in regional transit planning activities, and coordinates with the Arizona Department of Transportation and local governments for transportation related funding. Additionally, the agency develops, adopts and maintains an area-wide water quality management plan.

Contact Information

Web Address
https://nacog.org/
https://yavapaiatwork.com
Email: lcickavage@nacog.org
clyons@nacog.org
Telephone # 928-577-8142, 928-649-6867

New Trails Expansion in Camp Verde
The Town of Camp Verde Economic Development Department is fortunate to be able to partner with the Coconino National Forest's Red Rock Ranger District to make a 6-mile loop trail that will extends from the Sports Complex. With the help of a RAC grant and an AMAZING American Conservation Experience Crew. Happy Trails, fellow Camp Verdeans!
Web Address
https://www.fs.usda.gov/coconino

√ Phillip England Center for the Performing Arts

The Town of Camp Verde and the Verde Valley are fortunate to have the Phillip England Center for the Performing Arts to showcase the performing arts through musical, educational, and other artistic performances.

Contact Information

Web Address
https://www.pecpaf.org/
Face Book URL
https://www.facebook.com/pecpaf
Email: pecpaf@pecpaf.com
Telephone # 928-593-0364

Town of Camp Verde

* Local government offices and services.
  Information on permits
  Jobs
  Community Events
  Economic development
  Town meeting minutes and agenda
  Event calendar
  Parks and recreation

Face Book URL
https://www.facebook.com/TownOfCampVerde
Telephone # 928-554-0000

VFW POST 6739

277 Veterans Way
Camp Verde, AZ, 86322
The VFW exists to support those who have served in the military overseas during a conflict. The Camp Verde VFW is here for all veterans. **Contact Information**

Face Book URL
https://www.facebook.com/CampVerdeVFW6739/
Email: vfwpost6739@gmail.com
Telephone # 928-567-4642

Verde Independent Newspaper

Local news, sports, videos, photos from Cottonwood, Camp Verde, Clarkdale, Jerome, and other Verde Valley Arizona communities. As the community news source our comment profanity filter is set to "Strong" to hide foul language. Be courteous to be seen. 8:00 AM - 5:00 PM.

Contact Information

Read the Newspaper
http://verdenews.com/
Contact the Newspaper
https://www.verdenews.com/contact-us/
Telephone # 928-634-2241

COMMUNITY RESOURCES-SENIORS

Verde Valley Farmers Market

Saturdays Mid May to the first week in October, 8 am-noon. Hollamon and Main Camp Verde, AZ. Please bring your own bags or purchase one at the market and join us in our effort to be plastic-free. Buy local Eat fresh!

Contact Information

Face Book URL

https://www.facebook.com/
verdevalleyfarmersmarket

Email: jcdavie18@msn.com

Telephone # 928-634-7077

____

The Verde Valley Humane Society

1520 West Mingus Avenue, Cottonwood, Arizona 86326

The Verde Valley Humane Society's Adopt for Life Shelter is a non-profit organization developed to encourage a healthy pet population in our communities. We employ a stringent adoption policy in order to have successful adoptions into happy families. Our pets do not leave our facility without being spayed or neutered and have their shots or a certificate for shots and a free vet visit. Animals picked up as strays by Animal Control Officers may be retrieved during office hours. Please bring proof of spay/neuter and vaccinations. Fees and fines vary among our contractual partners. Please bring a leash and collar to retrieve your pet.

Contact Information

Web Address

http://www.verdevalleyhumanesociety.org/

Face Book URL

https://www.facebook.com/
HumaneSocietyVerdeValley/about/?ref=page_
internal

Email: frontdesk@verdevalleyhumanesociety.org

Telephone # 928-634-7387

____

Verde Valley Kayaker's Club

VVKC is a group of people of all ages and walks of life. We're no pros we're just everyday average people who love to kayak, paddle board or canoe. We don't care what your skill level is or if you've never been on the water. This is a place to share your trips, plan for future adventures, ask questions and provide insight.

HAVE FUN AND BE SAFE!!!!

Contact Information

Face Book URL

https://www.facebook.com/
groups/1630774143707038

Current conditions for the rising river:

https://waterdata.usgs.gov/az/nwis/uv/?site_
no=09506000&PARAmeter_cd=00065,00060

____

√ Verde Valley Sanctuary

The Verde Valley Sanctuary offers a safe haven for victims of family violence and sexual assault, providing shelter, community outreach, legal advocacy and education and prevention. If you or someone you know feels threatened, please contact us immediately. Services available in English and Spanish.

The Verde Valley Sanctuary is currently accepting donations Tuesday through Saturday 10-4 at their new thrift shop location located at 567 S. Main Street Camp Verde.

Contact Information

Web Address

https://verdevalleysanctuary.org/

Face Book URL

https://www.facebook.com/VerdeValleySanctuary

Email: development@verdevalleysanctuary.org

Telephone # 928-639-5772

COMMUNITY RESOURCES

Yavapai County Sheriff's Office

Law Enforcement Services for all of Yavapai County - Headquartered in Prescott, Arizona. THIS PAGE IS NOT MONITORED 24 HOURS A DAY. CALL 928-771-3260 OR 911 TO REPORT A CRIME.

Face Book URL

https://www.facebook.com/YavapaiCountySheriff

COTTONWOOD FOOD BANKS

7 DAYS A WEEK

Journey Church
750 E. Mingus Ave. Cottonwood, AZ 86326
(928)634-4321
Tuesday's 12pm-6pm
Mountain View United Methodist Church
901 S. 12thSt. Cottonwood, AZ 86326
(928)634-8857
New Hope Christian Fellowship
E. Villa Dr. Cottonwood, AZ 86326
928-634-4673
Sunday's 12pm-1pm
Mountain View United Methodist Church
901 S. 12thSt. Cottonwood, AZ 86326
928-634-8857
nd & 4th Wednesday of Each Month 8am-4pm
New Hope Christian Fellowship
E. Villa Dr. Cottonwood, AZ 86326
928-634-4673
Sunday's 12pm-1pm Tuesday's 11am-12pm
Friday's 11am-12pm
Old Town Mission
116 E. Pinal St. Cottonwood, AZ 86326
928-634-7869
Monday's 9am-2pm
Thursday's 9am-2pm
Project Rising Hope Food Pantry
750 E. Mingus Ave. Cottonwood, AZ 86326
Tuesday's 12pm-6pm
Saint Vincent De Paul
825 W Mingus Ave Cottonwood, AZ 86326
928-639-3000

Call the 1st Tuesday of the Month for food box pick up
Verde Valley Christian Church
406 S. 6th St. Cottonwood, AZ 86326
928-634-8166
Saturday's 8:30am-9:30am

Seniors
MEDICAL SERVICES IN OR NEAR CAMP VERDE

Angels Care

301 S. Willard Street, Cottonwood, AZ 86326
We provide skilled nursing care, restorative therapy and medical social services to patients in their homes or wherever they may reside, including assisted living facilities and retirement communities.

Contact Information
Web Address
https://www.angelscarehealth.com/
Telephone #   928-649-8890

Angels on Duty

155 South Montezuma Castle Hwy., #9
Camp Verde, Arizona 86322
Angels On Duty is a non-medical home care company that provides service to all of Arizona. Angels On Duty assists everyone of all ages and illnesses or disabilities with everyday tasks like going to the store, taking out the trash, remembering to take medications, preparing a simple meal, basic housekeeping chores, or transportation to doctor's appointments or social activities.

Contact Information
Web Address
https://www.angelsondutyhomecare.com/
Email: rosie.aod@gmail.com
Email: rhenkel.aod@gmail.com
Telephone # 928-567-8883

COMMUNITY RESOURCES-SENIORS

Bashes Senior Day

Take advantage of Bashas' Senior Discount Day! The first Wednesday of every month, customers 55 and older can save an additional 10% off their purchase in a single transaction. Customers may be asked to present ID for age verification and are required to use their Thank You Card to receive the Senior Discount. It's how Arizona's hometown grocer thanks Arizona seniors.

*Senior Discount is not eligible on prescriptions, alcoholic beverages, tobacco products, postage stamps, gift cards, Western Union, taxes, fuel or lottery tickets.

Contact Information

Web Address

https://www.bashas.com/senior-discount/

____

Camp Verde Community Library Classes for Seniors

The Camp Verde Community Library has several classes especially geared for seniors. Check out their calendar. Classes on Medicare, nutrition and wellness.

Contact Information

Web Address

https://www.campverde.az.gov/departments/community-library

Face Book URL

https://www.facebook.com/campverdelibrary

Email: library@campverde.az.gov

Telephone # 928-554-8380

____

Camp Verde Eye Care

452 W Finnie Flat Rd Suite A1, Camp Verde, Arizona 86322

Welcome to Camp Verde Eye Care, where we put your vision and well-being first. We invite you to peruse our company and eye care-related information. With over 50 years of experience in the optometry field, Dr. Jorge D. Huston is prepared for any medical situation and will make sure you are cared for with the best services.

Services:
- Eye Exams
- Optical Frames
- Dry-Eye Treatment
- Contact Lenses Services
- Specialty Eye Glass Lenses

Hours: Monday thru Friday 8-5 Closed 12-1 for lunch.

Contact Information

Web Address

https://www.cv-eyecare.com/

Face Book URL

Telephone # 928-567-3330

____

Camp Verde Family Chiropractic and Wellness Center
Wingfield Plaza

564 Main Street, Camp Verde, Az 86322

Thorough and individualized health care options. Chiropractic and Acupuncture. About the clinic: We are a small family-run chiropractic clinic serving Camp Verde and the surrounding Verde Valley since 2010. We strive to provide high-quality, individualized health care to all of our patients. Dr. French is continually seeking additional education to improve his skills and knowledge in an effort to always offer his patients the best quality care. Monday-Thursday: 8:00am-12pm and 2pm-5:00pm (closed from 12pm-2pm) Friday: 8:00am-12pm

Contact Information

Web Address

https://campverdechiropractor.com/

Face Book URL

https://www.facebook.com/CampVerdeChiropractic

Email: CampVerdeChiropractic@gmail.com

Telephone # Phone: 928-567-0202

Fax: 928-567-0303

____

Copper Canyon Family Dental
26 W Salt Mine Rd. Camp Verde, AZ 86322
Dr. Ryan Carter would like to thank you for stopping by. We are a full service dental practice for both children and adults which includes cosmetic and restorative dentistry. Establishing and maintaining the highest degree of oral health is the top priority for our patients. Copper Canyon Family Dentistry can improve your smile from simple whitening procedures to complete dental make overs.

-Cleanings and X-rays
-Children's dentistry
-Cosmetic dentistry services
-Veneers
-Tooth colored fillings
-Emergency treatment
-Crowns and bridges
-Treatment for gum disease
-Partial dentures
-Full dentures
-Teeth whitening
-Sleep apnea treatment

Contact Information
Web Address
https://coppercanyonfamilydental.com/
Face Book URL
https://www.facebook.com/
coppercanyonfamilydental/
Email: coppercanyonfamilydental@gmail.com
Telephone # 928-567-3306

Copper Canyon Medical Clinic
348 S Main St, Camp Verde, AZ 86322
Primary Medical Care MD
-Dinizio Jessica DO
-Joseph Oleo MA
-Rayburn Leo DC
-Dr. Ronald E. Parfitt, MD
Hours: Open 8AM -Closes 5PM

Contact Information
Telephone # 928-649-6477

√ Haven Health in Camp Verde
86 West Salt Mine Road,
Camp Verde, Arizona 86322
Haven Health in Camp Verde, Arizona, islocated in the heart of the Verde Valley between Cottonwood, Sedona and Prescott. Our Camp Verde Haven Health location offers a beautiful rehabilitation spa, serene and welcoming living areas and peaceful resident rooms for rest, relaxation and healing.
Our caring professionals are committed to providing the best skilled nursing, physical therapy, occupational therapy, speech language pathology, wound care and other rehabilitation services to help you or your loved one regain confidence, functionality and independence. Call our team today to learn more about our services or to schedule a tour of our Camp Verde care facility.

Contact Information
Web Address
https://www.havenhealthaz.com/locations/camp-verde/
Face Book URL
https://www.facebook.com/havenofcampverde
Email: edulas@havenhg.com
Telephone # 928-567-5253   928-567-3794
FAX: 928-239-9701

COMMUNITY RESOURCES-MEDICAL

Spectrum Healthcare Group

At Spectrum Healthcare Group we have one priority: You. Offering COVID-19 Vaccination, BIOTE, Primary Care, Behavioral Health, Pain Management, Substance Abuse Treatment, Virtual Service. Same Day Appointments. **The mobile crisis team** is staffed with specially trained crisis response specialists, and coordinates with Spectrum psychiatry, primary care providers, nurses, and counselors.
Same Day Appointments
Walk-Ins Welcome

Contact Information

Web Address
https://www.spectrumhealthcare-group.com/
Face Book URL
https://www.facebook.com/SpectrumHealthcare-Group/
Email: info@spectrumhealthcare-group.org
Telephone # 877-634-7333
To reach crisis services, call 928-634-2236
or the Northern AZ Crisis line at 877-756-4090
Cottonwood – Main
8 E Cottonwood St. Cottonwood, AZ 86326
Cottonwood – Mingus
651 W. Mingus Avenue Cottonwood, AZ 86326
Camp Verde
452 Finnie Flat Road Camp Verde, AZ 86322
Prescott – Crossings
3633 Crossings Dr.Prescott, AZ 86305
Prescott – Willow Creek
990 Willow Creek Rd. Prescott, AZ 86301

Verde Dental Care

Outpost Mall
522 Finnie Flat Rd J. Camp Verde, AZ 86322
Trusted and comfortable dental care. At Verde Dental Care, we have extensive experience in all aspects of modern dentistry. We offer comprehensive dental care, including everything from the preventive education & routine hygiene that help to reduce dental problems to expert solutions for the dental issues our patients face like orthodontics & restorative dentistry–all at one convenient Camp Verde dentist. Hours: Open8-Closes 6PM

Services:
Cosmetic Dentistry
Dental Implants
General Dentistry
Preventative Dentistry
We love kids and families

Contact Information

Web Address
https://verdedentalcare.com/
Face Book URL
https://www.facebook.com/VerdeDentalCare/
Email: contact@verdedentalcare.com
Telephone # 928-567-5249

Verde Smiles

Dr. Farhad Sharifi and his team in Camp Verde provide a full range of dental services, from Implant & Restorative Dentistry to Cosmetic Dentistry and Periodontics. We cater to patients who expect the highest level of care and service.

Contact Information

Web Address
https://verdesmiles.com/
Telephone # 928-567-3799

COMMUNITY RESOURCES-MEDICAL

Verde Valley Care Givers

299 Van Deren Road, Suite 2, Sedona, Arizona 86336
Our Vision: No Senior Left Isolated.
Our Mission: To provide accessible transportation and programs, through volunteer services, to support adults in need of assistance to maintain their independence and quality of life at home. Accolades: Named #1 in the nation for volunteer transportation in 2016.

Contact Information
Web Address
http://www.vvcaregivers.org/
Face Book URL
https://www.facebook.com/VVCC86/
Email: info@vvcaregivers.org
Telephone # 928-204-1238

Verde Valley Medical Clinic

1298 Finnie Flat Rd #101, Camp Verde, AZ 86322
Family practice physician in Camp Verde, Arizona Northern Arizona Healthcare Medical Group - Camp Verde provides a multidisciplinary primary care approach involving physicians, physician assistants and nurse practitioners to help you and your family stay healthy. We provide personalized care in a number of areas including:

Wellness exams.
Preventive healthcare and screening services.
Immunizations and vaccines. Our experienced staff can answer your questions and provide you with recommendations for any age.
Sports physicals for student athletes.
Pre-operative evaluation.
EKG.
Acute injury evaluation and treatment.
Minor dermatology, podiatry and other office procedures.
Evaluation and management of behavioral health conditions.

Visiting specialists including neurologists, cardiologists and endocrinologists.
Access to your confidential health records via the patient portal.
Convenient appointment times and extended hours

Hours: Open7- Closes 8PM
Contact Information
Web Address
https://www.nahealth.com/northern-arizona-healthcare-medical-group-camp-verde
Face Book URL
https://www.facebook.com/NAHVerdeValley/
Telephone # 928-639-5555

Yavapai Apache Health Center

Address: 2400 Datsi St. Camp Verde, AZ 86322
The Yavapai-Apache Nation is located in the Verde Valley of Arizona and is comprised of five (5) tribal communities: Tunlii, Middle Verde, Rimrock, Camp Verde and Clarkdale.
Contact Information
Web Address
https://yavapai-apache.org/
Telephone # 928-567-2168

Verde View Senior Apartments

377 W. General Crook Trail, Camp Verde, AZ 86322

Verde View Senior Apartments is an affordable, older adult (62+) community with several apartments equipped to accommodate those who are mobility impaired (available to those over the age of 18).

Our community is located within walking distance of pharmacies, grocery stores, and specialty stores. In town there are several restaurants, a post office, and a casino.

Medical facilities and services are located in Cottonwood, 15 miles away. Meals-On-Wheels and Adult Care are available upon request to our residents. Transportation is available by bus or taxi.

A Social Service Coordinator is available to help residents' find services for their personal needs. Pets are welcomed but require a deposit and have size limitations.

Verde View is a smoke-free community.

Studio & One Bedroom Apartments Include:
- Bathroom with Safety Features
- Full Kitchen (electric appliances)
- Individually Controlled Heat & Air Conditioning
- Emergency Call System
- Fire & Smoke Detectors
- Carpeting
- Window Treatments

Building Amenities Include:
- On-Site Laundry Room
- Individual Indoor Mailboxes
- Controlled Entry Access System
- Community Room
- Library
- Convenient to Public Transportation
- On-Site Management Staff
- On-Site Maintenance Staff
- Service Coordinator on Staff

Contact Information
Web Address
https://www.rhf.org/location/verde-view/
Face Book URL
https://www.facebook.com/
RetirementHousingFoundation/
Email: info@rhf.org
Telephone # tel 928-567-9378
fax 928-567-9379

MILITARY VETERANS

American Legion Post 93
286 S 3rd St. Camp Verde, AZ 86322
The American Legion was chartered and incorporated by Congress in 1919 as a patriotic veterans organization devoted to mutual helpfulness. Benefits, career, health, troop and family support, USAA Financial Center, Women Veterans, Scholarships.

Contact Information
Web Address
https://www.legion.org/
Face Book URL
https://www.facebook.com/
DavidCJohnsonAmerlegionPost93
Telephone # 928-567-6154

US Veterans Administration Services

Government Office
Old Town Shops
Address: 123 N San Francisco St.
Flagstaff, AZ 86001
Contact Information
Web Address
https://www.va.gov/
Telephone # 928-226-1844

VFW Post 6739 in Camp Verde

377 W State Route 260, Camp Verde, AZ 86322
Veterans organization. Promoting community, advocacy, assistance. The VFW Podcast, Health & Fitness for Physical, Mental, and Emotional Well-being.

Contact Information
Web Address
https://www.vfw.org/
Face Book URL
https://www.facebook.com/CampVerdeVFW6739/
Email: vfwpost6739@gmail.com
Telephone # 928-567-4642

Business

→Downtown Camp Verde

A.I.D. Development Inc

Construction & Contractors; Digging and Excavating, grading, augering, concrete breaking, demo and haul off, brush and field mowing, Hauling: I can haul practically any type of material from 1 ton to 20 tons. Dirt – sand – gravel - aggregate – decorative rock – boulders and almost anything else that fits in the dump bed.

One of my dump trucks has a special "high lift" tailgate so hauling large odd-shaped materials/debris is no problem. Call, text or email me for hauling quotes.

Contact Information
Face Book URL
https://www.vvdirtwork.com/
Email: Not Available
Telephone # 928-300-4578

AAA Mini Storage

555 S 1St St, Camp Verde Az 86322
Spare Foot is the largest on-line marketplace for Self-storage with direct access to the largest volume of high-quality storage statistics in the industry. That allows us to give you the most comprehensive outlook on storage trends across the country and in Arizona.

Contact Information
Face Book URL
https://www.facebook.com/aaastoragesedona/
Telephone # 928-567-3310

Reserved add space for Chamber adds.

Call to reserve space. Must be a member.

1/4 Page $100, 1/2 Page $200, Full Page $400

Reserved add space for Chamber adds.

Call to reserve space. Must be a member.

1/4 Page $100, 1/2 Page $200, Full Page $400

Camp Verde Business-Downtown

AB Massage

564 S Main St #110a, Camp Verde AZ 86322
We are a massage studio of massage Therapists ready to assist in your health and wellness. We can help you simply relax or help you with complex medical conditions that are limiting your range of motion. We have two locations in the Verde Valley to serve you. Cottonwood and Camp Verde. Mon-Sun 8A-8P

Contact Information

Web Address
https://abmassageaz.com/
Telephone # 928-235-8821

Ability Repair LLC

492 Yaqui Cir., Camp Verde, Az 86322
I service and repair Air Conditioning, Refrigeration, and Appliance.   This includes Recreational Vehicle Rooftop Air Conditioning. Gas Range and Dryers conversion from natural gas to propane. I may be able to design and build automatic controls and or remote controls for your equipment. I service the Verde Valley are including Sedona, VOC, Rimrock, Cornville, Camp Verde, Cottonwood, Clarkdale and Jerome.

Contact Information

Web Address
https://www.abilityrepair.com/
Face Book URL
https://www.facebook.com/ABILITYFIX/
Email: Stevebeach@gmail.com
Telephone # 928-300-7898

√ Ace Hardware Camp Verde

285 S. Main, Camp Verde AZ 86322
We are open at our physical location as well as accepting online/instore pickup orders on www.acehardware.com phone orders and curbside delivery. We are open Mon.-Fri. 7:30 a.m. - 5:00 p.m. Sat. 8:00 a.m. - 5:00 p.m. Sun. 9:00 a.m. - 3:00 p.m. We are also actively running our rental department.

Contact Information

Web Address
https://www.acehardware.com
Telephone # 928-567-4172

All About You Hair Studio

545 S. Main Street #1, Camp Verde AZ 86322
Haircuts for Men and Women. Chemicals (Perms, highlights, all over colors, specialty colors etc.) For appointment Mon 9A-2P. Tues-Fri 9A-5P, Sat 9A-2P

Contact Information

Face Book URL
https://www.facebook.com/All-About-You-Hair-Studio-1503982536499802/
Telephone # 928-567-6800

Alternative Blue Print

93 Arnold St. Camp Verde AZ 86322
Engineering copies, computer plotting, full-size scanning. Web Design.

Contact Information

Web Address
https://www.alternative-blueprint.com/
Email: printmaster@alternative-blueprint.com
Telephone # 928-567-4949

Camp Verde Business-Downtown

American Heritage Academy

132 General Crook Trail, Camp Verde, AZ 86322
Building tomorrow's heroes today. Public
Elementary School grades 1-12. 165 Students.
Charter School.

Contact Information

Web Address
https://ahacottonwood.org/
Telephone # 928-567-0462

Anasazi Creations Jewelry

630 Dakota Dr., Camp Verde Az 86322
Susan Shatreau-Janisky a Metis of French
Canadian, Algonquin, Mohawk & Scottish
ancestry is a registered member of the Aboriginal
Metis Community of Maniwaki, Quebec, Canada.

She was born in northern upstate New York
and has resided in California & Arizona. Susan
presently resides in Northern Arizona with her
husband Michael Janisky. Susan is an award-
winning artist, her artworks have been in several
types of native art mediums over a many year
span including silversmithing, wire art, leather &
beadwork using traditional designs passed down
through her relations & her own contemporary
creations. Her specialties are custom made
medicine bags beaded on native tanned smoked
deer skin & beaded cuff bracelets, elk & deer sking
cross body bags.

Contact Information

Face Book URL
https://www.facebook.com/
AnasaziCreationsJewelryDesignLlc/
Telephone # 928-550-2181

Arizona Central Land and Home

348 S. Main St. Ste. 5, Camp Verde, AZ 86322
For Mail: PO BOX 4681, Camp Verde, AZ 86322
Real Estate, Free property evaluation, view
properties for sale in the local area. Serving Camp
Verde, Rimrock, Lake Montezuma, Cottonwood,
Cornville, and Sedona Arizona. For Appointment
or showing.

Contact Information

Web Address
https://outstandingagents.com/
Face Book URL
https://www.facebook.com/azcentral
Telephone # 928-567-0770

√ Arizona Parks and Recreation

395 South Main Street, Camp Verde, AZ 86322
The Town of Camp Verde Parks and Recreation
Department is dedicated to providing quality
recreational, educational, cultural, fitness, social,
and environmental opportunities that meet the
diverse needs of our community.
Hours: Mon – Thur 7A– 5P, Fri 7A–1

Contact Information

Web Address
https://www.campverde.az.gov/departments/parks-
recreation
Email: Parks@campverde.az.gov
Telephone # 928-554-0828
FAX 928-567-1540

Camp Verde Business-Downtown

Arts Alliance of Camp Verde

The Arts Alliance of Camp Verde supports an inclusive arts community by connecting artists to creative opportunities.

Contact Information

Face Book URL

https://www.facebook.com/ArtsAllianceofCV

E-Mail: artsallianceofcampverde@gmail.com

Aspen RV

1351 E Winchester Trail, Camp Verde, AZ
Convenient & Easy RV Repairs at your location. Most RV Repair Shops are booked several weeks out, which means long wait times for you or even a cancellation of your trip. With Aspen RV you don't need to wait, we make it easy and convenient because we are mobile and come to you.

Repair of most RV Systems and Components, Emergency Repairs,Routine Maintenance, Winterization/De-winterization, Maintenance Evaluations,Inspections, Owner Orientations, Consulting.

Don't let an issue with your RV ruin your vacation or disrupt your life, let Aspen RV make repairs and maintenance simple for you. Service Areas Aspen RV Serves the entire Verde Valley to include Camp Verde, Cottonwood, Sedona. We also provide service in Prescott Valley, Prescott and surrounding areas, Flagstaff, Payson, Happy Jack, Mormon Lake, and many more areas.

Contact Information

Web Address

https://www.aspenrvrepair.com/

Face Book URL

https://www.facebook.com/Aspen-RV-Mobile-Services-835856020128891

Email: justin@aspenrvrepair.com

Telephone # 928-683-5522

Ben Roti Ceramics

2175 S. Glenrose Drive, Camp Verde, AZ 86322
Open by appointment.
Ceramic throwing classes offered. 4-week classes and private classes are offered. Small class sizes, one-on-one instruction.

Contact Information

Telephone # 520-400-4522

Bill Ralston Construction LLC

2877 S Salt Mine Road, Camp Verde, AZ
We are a bonded general contractor that offers green building, design build services and other services.

Contact Information

Web Address

https://local.yahoo.com/info-216481042-bill-ralston-construction-company-camp-verde;_ylt=Awr9Eem4Y_lhOZIAOY3umYlQ;_

29sbwNncTEEcG9zAzEEdnRpZAMEc2VjA3Nj

Email: Not Available

Telephone # 928-203-9559

Bueler Funeral Home

143 East Arnold St. Camp Verde, AZ 86322
Bueler funeral home and crematory serve Verde Valley family and friends with respect and integrity. On-line tributes. Pre-planning, grief support, traditional funerals and cremation services. Open 24 hr.

Contact Information

Web Address

https://buelerfuneralhome.com/

Telephone # 928-567-5206

FAX 928-567-9176

Camp Verde Business-Downtown

Bullard Construction Company

Camp Verde, AZ
Since 1950, Bullard Construction Co (inc)
has been providing Single-family Housing
Construction in Camp Verde.

Contact Information
Web Address
http://bullardinc.net/
Face Book URL
https://www.facebook.com/bullardinc
Email: bryan@bullardinc.net
Telephone # 928-254-9381

CD Outdoors

556 S. Azure Dr. Camp Verde AZ 86322
Pack Rafts, kayaks, paddles, PFD, dog PFD, dry
bags, tents. Call for Appointment.
Contact Information
Web Address
https://www.cdoutdoors.net/
Email: carlos@cdoutdoors.net
Telephone # 602-750-4850   602-690-7223

Caditt LLC

757 W. Azure Dr
CAD Designer
Contact Information
Email: areta.arizona@gmail.com
Telephone # 928-554-4589

Camp Verde Barbers

270 Main St. Camp Verde, AZ 86322
Hair Cuts $12 (Includes Tax. Cash Only.)
Please follow COVID guidelines. Barbers are
Gary, Johnny, and Cecil. Walk-in Only. Hours
Tues-Fri 9A-5P

Camp Verde Bicycle

735 S. Main Street, Camp Verde AZ 86322
Regular Hours (Thurs-Sat 10A-6P)
Mountain bikes, BMX, Cruisers, Sales and
Service. Call for an appointment.
Contact Information
Web Address
https://flagstaffbicycle.com/
Email: jcsrecyclery@gmail.com
Telephone # 928-567-6734

Camp Verde Bugle

116 S. Main St. Cottonwood
Camp Verde Bugle, Verde Independent, Verde
Valley Newspapers
Contact Information
Web Address
https://www.verdenews.com/news/camp-verde-bugle/
Telephone # 928-634-2241, 928-567-4101

Camp Verde Business-Downtown

√ Camp Verde Chamber & Business Alliance

(Mail) 522 Finnie Flat Rd. #179 Camp Verde, AZ 86322

CVCBA is a dynamic network dedicated to the prosperity of businesses-new and old, small or large--in Camp Verde and throughout the Verde Valley. We honor the rich heritage of our community and enthusiastically support future development. We are committed to providing representation, promotion, and resources for the business community.

Contact Information

Web Address
https://campverdebiz.com/
Face Book URL
https://www.facebook.com/campverdechamber
Email: cvcbacampverde@gmail.com
Telephone # 928-203-6863

Camp Verde Dance and Fitness

564 S. Main St #113, Camp Verde AZ 86322
Wingfield Plaza
Twinkle toes ballet, lyrical modern dance, yoga, Pilates, cycle, kickboxing, silver sneakers, and more. M-F 8A-7P, Sat 8A-12PM Call for hours and classes.

Contact Information

Web Address
https://campverdedanceandfitness.com/
Email: campverdedanceandfitness@yahoo.com
Telephone # 928-499-2619

Camp Verde Feed & Country Store

584 S. Main St. Camp Verde AZ 86322
Hunting and fishing supplies, bait, ammo, licenses and equipment, pet feed and supplies, horse shoes, electric fencing, tack, beer, wine, fertilizer, liquor, propane. Drive-Through or walk in store. Hours Mon-Sat 6A-8P, Sun 7A-8P.

Contact Information

Web Address
http://campverdefeedstore.com/
Face Book URL
https://www.facebook.com/CVFeedstore/
Email: campverdefeedstore@gmail.com
Telephone # 928-567-3351

Camp Verde Reality

295 S. Main St. Camp Verde AZ 86322
Welcome to the premier resource for all real estate information and services in the area. Looking for a new home? You can browse an up-to-date database list of all available properties in the area, or we will conduct a personalized search for you. Free market analysis for home sales. Call for an Appointment. Hours M-F 9A-5P, Sat 9A-3P.

Contact Information

Web Address
https://www.campverderealty.com/
Face Book URL
https://www.facebook.com/
CampVerdeRealtySellsHomes
Telephone # 928-567-6474

Sales Associates

Barbara Parsons -Sales Associate
Email: Parsonsfamily4@msn.com
Telephone # 928-821-0955 (Cell Phone)

Bridgett Bowers- Sales Associate/Property Management
Telephone # 928-300-2533 (Cell Phone)

Dianna Stevens -Sales Associate
Email: dianna_stevens@msn.com

Camp Verde Business-Downtown

Telephone # 928-567-6474 (Office Phone)
928-607-7677 (Cell Phone)

Bill Carter Designated Broker Sedona Verde Valley Association of Realtors
Telephone # 9285676474

Camp Verde Senior Center

263 Maryvale Drive, Camp Verde AZ 86322
Amenities for our members include: Pool table, board games, puzzles, and computer access.

Visit our Book Nook
Our Book Nook is located in the thrift store where books are for sale! Pick up your favorite books and join us upstairs in our Library where you can read while you are there. There is always a puzzle to be worked on in the dining room!
There are also games - CD's - DVD's etc.

Lunch Served Monday thru Friday at 11:30am
Our meals are made fresh each day and include: soup, salad, vegetables, a main entrée, desert and drinks (coffee, tea, and water). The price is $6.00 per member and $7.00 for non-member.
You don't have to be a member or certain age to eat a great meal here, Everyone is Welcome!!
Contact Information
Web Address
https://cvseniorcenter.weebly.com/
Face Book URL
https://www.facebook.com/The-Camp-Verde-Senior-Center-Thrift-Store-941773319179480
Email: cvazseniorcenter@outlook.com
Telephone # 928-567-6356

Camp Verde Water System

499 S. 6th St. Camp Verde, AZ 86322
Monthly payments are being made via their drop box in front of the office.
Contact Information
Telephone # 928-567-5281

Center State Equipment

245 Head St. Camp Verde, AZ 86322
Restaurant Equipment and Supplies.
Contact Information
Telephone # 928-567-3433

Chambers Realty Group

Wingfield Plaza
564 S. Main Street Suite 105, Camp Verde AZ 86322
Please call Chambers Realty Group if you are looking to buy or sell property in Camp Verde where our office is located in the historical Wingfield Plaza at 564 S. Main Street Suite 105. We pride ourselves on providing to our clients unparalleled services when buying or selling real estate in the Camp Verde and Verde Valley. We will provide a home warranty to any buyer of your property when you list with us, saving you on average about 500 dollars. We are open weekdays from 8 am until 5 pm. We are open on weekends by appointment.
Contact Information
Face Book URL
https://www.facebook.com/ChambersRealtyGroupLLC
Email: ucjustinchambers@gmail.com
Telephone # 928-718-2020

Camp Verde Business-Downtown

Classic Frame
31 W. Hollomon St., Camp Verde AZ 86322
John Wisniewski
Framing, matting pictures
M-F 9:30A-5P
Contact Information
Web Address
https://classicpictureframing.com/
Email: email: johnnycat@q.com
Telephone # 9285679544

Copper Canyon Family Health Center
348 S. Main St.
Family Medical Practice. Call for Appointment.
Contact Information
Telephone # 928-649-6477

Cowboy Corner
573 S. Main Street, Camp Verde AZ 86322
Saddle and Tack Shop.
(Store) Bits and spurs, breast collars, chaps, headstalls, pads and blankets, reins, saddles, training equipment. Buy, sell and trade.
Mon-Sat 10A-5P For appointment call.
Contact Information
Web Address
http://www.cowboycorner-az.com/
Telephone # 928-567-6699

Camp Verde Council Woman

Jackie Baker

√ Council Woman Jackie Baker
The Town of Camp Verde operates under the Council/Manager form of government. Legislative authority is vested in the seven-member town council which includes a voting mayor, vice-mayor, and five council members.
Contact Information
Web Address
https://www.campverde.az.gov/departments/town-council

Crystal Lattice Funky Market & Gifts
348 S Main St, Camp Verde, AZ 86322
Inside Verde Valley Resale & Consignment.
Wellness, Essential Oils, 20,000 Secrets of Tea, Book, CC Pollen Propolis Elderberry Spray Incense, Sage & Smudging Herbs, Sterling Silver Gemstone Jewelry.
Contact Information
Web Address
https://www.crystal-lattice.com/Default.asp
Email: admin@crystal-lattice.com
Telephone # 928-567-1212

CV Electric LLC
246 W Salt Mine Rd, Camp Verde, AZ 86322
Dalton's A/C, Heating and Refrigeration LLC
We offer A/C Installation, Air Duct Installation, Boiler Services, Electric Furnace Installation, A/C Repair, Air Duct Repair, Ductless A/C Services, Electric Furnace Repair Emergency Services, Gas Furnace Installation, Heater Installation, Thermostat Repair, Flame Sensor Repair, Gas Furnace Repair, Heater Repair.
Contact Information
Web Address
https://daltonac.net/
Email: None available
Telephone # 928-592-9146

Camp Verde Business-Downtown

√ Dog Tags

593 South Park Circle, Camp Verde AZ 86322
Professional Author; Historical Novels, war novels, children's book.

Contact Information

Web Address for Author
https://www.amazon.com/
s?k=wayne+treptow&ref=nb_sb_noss_2
Email: vikwayaz1@gmail.com
Telephone # 602-781-8025

Dreamy's Sewing & Alterations

365 S 4th St.
Sewing and Alterations. Wed-Sat 10A-4P

Contact Information

Telephone # 928-567-8712 928-567-8211

El Centro Latino

Please call for new location. Small business book keeping, taxes, accounting, notary services, business consultation, audit representation. M-Tue 11A-5P, Wed 2P-8:30P, Th-Fri 9A-8:30P

Contact Information

Web Address
https://el-centro-latino.com/
Face Book URL
https://www.facebook.com/Ecltaxes/
Email: elcentrolatino@hotmail.com
Telephone # 928-592-0201

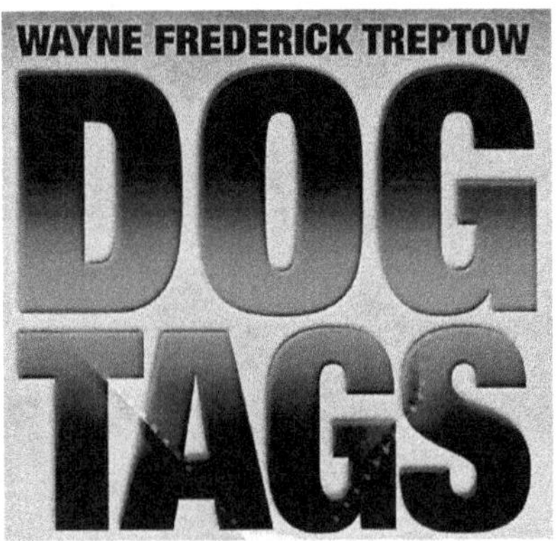

Expert Carpet & Upholstery Cleaning

346 3rd St.Camp Verde AZ 86322
Full range of services including, Carpet cleaning, upholstery cleaning, oriental rug cleaning, tile and grout cleaning. 24 Hour Emergency Service Flood/ Water Damage, RV /Motorhome, Mattress Cleaning, Black Light Mapping, Air Space Deodorizing, Dupont Teflon Carpet and Fabric Protectors. Call for an appointment. We don't cut corners; We clean them.

Contact Information

Web Address
https://expertcarpetandupholsterycleaning.com/
services
Telephone # 928-567-7334 Verde Valley, 928-282-3836 Sedona, 928-772-2928 Prescott

---

Express Automotive

673 S. 1st St. Camp Verde AZ 86322
Welcome to Express Automotive, your car service in Cottonwood and Camp Verde, AZ! We treat our auto repair professionals well because we value their skill and can-do attitude. When it comes to auto repair in Cottonwood, we are totally confident that Express Automotive is the best option in town!

Contact Information

Web Address
https://expressautomotivecottonwood.com
Telephone #
928-862-2572 Camp Verde
928-316-1053 Cottonwood

Camp Verde Business-Downtown

Fort River Auto Glass

675 S Main St. Camp Verde, AZ 86322
ADAS, calibration done on site. Windshield Chip repair. Windshield replacement.

Contact Information

Face Book URL
https://www.facebook.com/pages/category/
Automotive-Glass-Service/FORT-RIVER-AUTO-
GLASS-108658167540075/
Email: fortriverag@gmail.com
Telephone # 928-301-5287

Fort Verde Laundromat

348 South Main St. Camp Verde, AZ
Self serve wash and dry. Open 24 Hr.

Contact Information

Telephone # 928-821-0670

√ Fort Verde State Historical Park

125 E Hollamon St. Camp Verde, AZ 96322
Scenic 10-acre park featuring restored 19th century buildings, exhibits & occasional re-enactments. Fort Verde State Historic Park attempts to preserve parts of the Apache Wars-era fort as it appeared in the 1880s. The park was established in 1970. Open 7 day/week 10am-4pm.

Contact Information

Web Address
https://azstateparks.com/
Face Book URL
https://www.facebook.com/FortVerdeSHP/
Telephone # 928-567-3275

Fort Verde Suites

528 S. Main St. Camp Verde AZ 86322
Fort Verde Suites is locally owned and operated and is the ONLY hotel located on Historic Main Street in Downtown Camp Verde, Arizona. OPEN. New Hours 9 am-8 pm. We offer AAA, Military, Weekly and Monthly discounts. We have a picnic area equipped with tables, grill and horseshoes!

Contact Information

Web Address
https://www.fvsuites.com/
Face Book URL
https://www.facebook.com/FortVerdeSuites/
Telephone # 928-567-0275

Get Hitched Kwick

Mobile Marriage Service located in Camp Verde. Offices located in the city of Maricopa/Casa Grande and Camp Verde/Sedona. We will work with you to create a ceremony that is inspirational, personal and memorable. As Non-denominational ordained Ministers we support marriage equality and honor all religions. We will be happy to perform your Civil, religious, non-religious, elopement, interfaith, same sex, handfasting or prison ceremony. Belinda Clifford ULC & AMM certified Wedding Officiant and Notary Public.

Contact Information

Web Address
https://www.gethitchedkwik.com/
Face Book URL
https://www.facebook.com/GetHitchedKwik/
Email: gethitched@yahoo.com
Telephone # 520-568-9315

Camp Verde Business-Downtown

√ Glorybound Publishing

439 S. 6th St. Camp Verde AZ
Publishing first time authors as well as those working on their next book. Amazon, KDP, Printing, and binding. Amazon Campaign Manager. We specialize in not only publishing your book, but helping you to sell it. 9-5 by Appointment. Zoom appointments available. Appointments can be set up via the website if desired.

Contact Information
Web Address
https://gloryboundpublishing.com/
Face Book URL
https://www.facebook.com/gloryboundpublishing/?ref=bookmarks
Email: sheri@gloryboundpublishing.com
Telephone # 928-567-3340

√ Hair by Maya

365 S Main St. Suite 6 (inside Main Street Studios) Camp Verde, AZ 86322
Maya combines individualized attention & superior styling skills to create your dream hair. Maya specializes in personalized hair cutting, gentle haircolor, original Brazilian Blowout treatments, & dry-cutting for curly cuts and unique hair growth patterns. To make an appointment, contact Maya at 805.403.9121

Contact Information
Web Address
https://www.hairbymaya.com/
Telephone # 8054039121

Heritage Land Survey & Eng

738 S Parks Dr. Camp Verde, AZ 86322
Accurate, reliable, and responsive land surveying services.
Contact Information
Web Address
https://heritage-ls.com/
Telephone # 928-567-9170

Hollamon Generations Rd Boring

285 E Hollamon St, Camp Verde, AZ 86322
Drilling & Boring, demolition Contractor
Contact Information
Email: None Available
Telephone # 928-567-6208

√ Hope Women's Center

77 General Crook Trail, Camp Verde AZ 86322
We do this through a multitude of FREE, confidential services and programs which include:
• 1:1 Mentoring and Support Groups
• Parenting classes
• Life Skills and Faith Based Education Classes
• Grief Support and Celebrate Recovery
• Rise Above Abuse and Anger Management Classes
• Classes for birth moms with children in Foster Care or at risk of DCS removal
• Pregnancy Testing and Prenatal Classes
• ROSES Program for Pregnant Moms & Moms of Newborns (reducing Postpartum Depression)
• Specialized Maternal Mental Health support
• Childcare (0-5) for mothers attending Hope programs*
• Hope Heals - Crisis Counseling & Support
• Hope at Work - Job Skills Classes/Training
• Maternity Home for pregnant and parenting moms
• Points earned for programs can be used for Material Assistance such as utilities**, transportation, food, clothing, personal care items, household items, and baby/child products.

Camp Verde Business-Downtown

Contact Information
Web Address
https://hopewomenscenter.org/
Face Book URL
https://www.facebook.com/abidematernityhome/
Email: Info@AbideMaternityHome.com
Telephone #
928-567-5433
928-713-7007 after hours
8007124357 Pregnancy option **HOTLINE**

____

Inspired Gunworks LLC
735 South Azure Drive, Camp Verde, AZ 86322
Gunsmithing, sales, and soon-to-be Cerakote applicator. We have firearms, ammo, and optics for sale.
Contact Information
Face Book URL
https://www.facebook.com/amy.e.johnson.96
Email: Not Available
Telephone # 928-300-9306

____

Insurer's Network LTD.
Moving to a new building--please call for location Insurance bonds, your agency for auto, home, health, and life. 8A-4:30P Mon-Fri.
Closed Saturday and Sunday
Contact Information
Telephone # 928-567-4127

____

Hair By Maya

√ Integrated Therapeutic Mobile Massage
Mobile Massage by Heather Barton. Heather is a licensed LMT graduating from the Sedona School of Massage. She practices a variety of massage techniques. Call Heather for an appointment.
Contact Information
Telephone # 541-253-1961

____

√ JT's Bistro
348 S. Main St.
Great food, local wine, craft beers
5 star chef. Dine-in, take-out. Pet Friendly outdoor tables.
Contact Information
Web Address
https://www.jtsbistro.com/
Face Book URL
https://www.facebook.com/Jtbistro/
Email: info@jtsbistro.com
Telephone # 928-567-7520

____

Joel Westervelt Architect
93 Arnold St. Camp Verde AZ 86322
Arizona AIA Architect Offering Residential Design, Commercial Design & Planning. Specializing in Sedona Vernacular Architecture and Farmhouse Design. By Appointment.
Contact Information
Web Address
https://www.joelwesterveltarchitect.com/
Face Book URL
https://www.facebook.com/
JoelWesterveltArchitect
Email: email: jw@joelweterveltarchitect.com
Telephone # 928-567-2255

____

Camp Verde Business-Downtown

Joshua Tree Landscape

682 S. Main St. Camp Verde
(mail) PO Box 4462, Camp Verde, AZ
Landscape design, maintenance, tree care, tree
removal, lighting design and installation, retaining
walls, certified aquatic contractor, interlocking
brick specialist, concrete paver instillation,
certified arborist. By Appointment.
Contact Information
Web Address
https://www.joshuatreescape.com/
Email: joshuatreescape@gmail.com
Telephone #
928-567-4064 Verde Valley
928-204-1408   Sedona
928-778-6116 Prescott
928-774-2662 Flagstaff
Fax: (928)567-9388

√ Kiwanis Camp Verde

P.O. 974, Camp Verde AZ 86322
Non-profit philanthropic whose focus is child
related events. Dedicate to improving our
community one child at a time.
Contact Information
Face Book URL
https://www.facebook.com/Camp-Verde-Kiwanis-
Club-254686084991144/
Telephone # 928-567-3010

Kiwanis Clothes Closet

3095 E Beaver Creek Rd, Rimrock, AZ 86335
Monday   Closed

Tuesday   10AM–3PM

Wednesday   10AM–3PM

Thursday   10AM–3PM

Friday Closed

Saturday   10AM–3PM

Sunday Closed
Telephone # 928- 300-6072

Kocisko Construction

1000 W D Lane, Camp Verde, AZ 86322
Construction and general contractor.
Contact Information
Telephone # (928) 567-8702

La Casita

37 W. Hollamon St.
First-class Mexican cuisine. Serves alcohol.
10A-9P Every Day
Dine-in, on the porch or Take Out available
Contact Information
Face Book URL
https://www.facebook.com/La-
Casita-240420636160416
Telephone # 928-567-3202
10A-9P Every Day
Dine-in, on the porch or Take Out available

Laid Back Jewelry

567 S. Main St. Camp Verde AZ 86322
Call Jim for an appointment
Contact Information
Web Address
http://laidbackaz.weebly.com/
Telephone # 928-300-4309, 928-592-3993

Camp Verde Business-Downtown

Low Places Bar and Grill

Wingfield Plaza
564 S. Main St. Ste 100
Bar and Grill
Mon-Thur 11-10PM, Fri-Sat 11P-2A
Dine-in, Take-Out

Contact Information
Web Address
https://www.lowplacesbarandgrill.com/
Face Book URL
https://www.facebook.com/LowPlacesCV
Email: shannalee@lowplacesbarandgrill.com
Telephone # 928-567-8722

Lori's Lookin Good Hair Design

567 S. Main St. Camp Verde
9A-8P Mon-Sat , Call for an appointment.

Contact Information
Face Book URL
https://www.facebook.com/
Hairbenders6641/?rf=167173649964383
Telephone # 928-567-1255

Lucas Tactical Manufacturing
Lucas Tactical & Pawn

567 S Main Street Camp Verde, AZ 86322
Mailing: P.O. Box 2637 Camp Verde AZ 86322
Guns, jewelry, unique antiques and collectibles,
Native American artifacts, we have all of these
things and more for sale! We will also gladly give
you a loan on any items like that you have! come
see us today.

Contact Information
Email: pjonas2@msn.com
Telephone # 928-202-6899

√ Main Street Studios

365 Main St. Camp Verde AZ 86322
Located in downtown Camp Verde, you'll find our
gift gallery full of unique and beautiful gifts. In
every nook and corner, you'll discover wonderful
treasures that have been lovingly handcrafted by
our family. Handmade Folk art, Turquoise, and
silver jewelry.

Contact Information
Web Address
https://www.mainstreetstudioscampverde.com/
https://www.cfavour.com/
http://www.teresadelrito.com/
Face Book URL
https://www.facebook.com/teresadelrito/
Email: mainstreetstudioscb@gmail.com
Telephone # 505-982-8763

√ Magic Wok

348 S. Main St. Camp Verde, AZ - 86322
Welcome to MAGIC WOK KITCHEN & BAR.
John Teah, Magic Wok Chef and proprietor
invites you to enjoy a truly unique Asian dining
experience. We offer a sensational selection of
seasonal dishes consisting of fresh, locally grown,
hand-selected ingredients.
Hours: Open Thur - Mon 11am - 8pm.
Closed Tue & Wed Sun 11am-5pm

Contact Information
Web Address
https://magicwokaz.com/
Face Book URL
Email: info@magicwokaz.com
Telephone # 928-567-2418

Camp Verde Business-Downtown

Medicare Solutions

Camp Verde
Greg Matheny.
Independent Medicare Broker. Contact me for any
or all of your Medicare needs. Call, email, or text
Available by appointment. Virtual or in-person.

Contact Information

Face Book URL
www.facebook.com/mathenyproducers
Email: Mathenyproducers@outlook.com
Telephone # 928-377-8966

Melode's Grooming

434 Main St. Camp Verde, AZ 86322
Pet grooming. Your Best Friend's Best Friend. Call
for hours.

Contact Information

Email: melodeefrisch@hotmail.com
Telephone # 928-567-3932

Memories IT

434 S. Main #3, Camp Verde AZ 86322
Ira Piper
Network support and maintenance, IT Support and
video backup and digitization, Computer repair.
M-F 10A-5P Call for an appointment.

Contact Information

Web Address
https://memoriesit.com/
Face Book URL
https://www.facebook.com/MemoriesITcv/
Email: email: tech@memoriesit.com
Telephone # 928-239-5317

Michelle Lee Photography

545 S Main Street, Suite B, Camp Verde AZ 86322
Specializing in High School senior pictures,
newborns, weddings, and portrait photography.
Call for an appointment.

Contact Information

Web Address
https://www.michelleleephotographyaz.com/
Face Book URL
https://www.facebook.com/
michelleleecphotography/
Email: mleephotoaz@gmail.com
Telephone # 928-300-4372

Montezuma Veterinary Service

298 W. General Crook Trail
If your pet is sick or injured and in need of an
appointment, please call to schedule. Hours M-F
8A-5P Sat 8A-2P. Closed Sunday.

Contact Information

Web Address
https://www.montezumavet.com/
Face Book URL
https://www.facebook.com/profile.
php?id=100057350362374
Telephone # 928-567-5515

√ Mystic Muse

365 Main Street, Camp Verde AZ 86322
Unique gifts, crystals, and more. Classes and
psychic readings. Your soul's connection.

Contact Information

Web Address
https://www.mysticmuseonline.com/
Face Book URL
https://www.facebook.com/MysticMuseOnline
Email: mysticmuse5d@outlook.com
Telephone # 928-399-9230

Camp Verde Business-Downtown

Mr. Rooter Plumbing

248 General Crook Trail, Camp Verde AZ 86322
Commercial and residential plumbing. Broken or leaking pipes, clogged drains and sinks, tubs and showers and toilets. Broken-leaking water heaters or other plumbing appliances. Clogged or malfunctioning septic tanks.

Contact Information

Web Address
https://www.mrrooter.com/

Face Book URL
https://www.facebook.com/
MrRooterPlumbingPrescott

Telephone # Ph 888-861-4344 for a 24/7 Emergency plumbing problem.

Nails by Dani

567 S. Main St. Camp Verde, AZ

Contact Information

Web Address
https://www.groupon.com/biz/camp-verde-az/
signatures-nails-by-dani

Telephone # 928-821-0037 928-567-5105

√ New Life Thrift and Gift

77 General Crook Trail, Camp Verde AZ 86322
We have everything from books to boots, toys to tools, clothing to cookware, plus furniture and other fun stuff. Come shop Tuesdays through Saturdays from 9am to 5pm. New or gently used donations are appreciated and accepted on Tuesdays through Saturdays between 9am and 3pm. All proceeds benefit mamas and babies in our community. Sponsored by Hope Women's Center.

Contact Information

Web Address
https://hopewomenscenter.org/

Face Book URL
https://www.facebook.com/newlifethriftshopcv/

Email: Info@AbideMaternityHome.com

Telephone # 928-567-7325

√ NRL Mortgage

567 S. Main Street #G, Camp Verde AZ 86322
John Smoley
Mortgage financing, purchase, and refinance. Specializing with first-time home buyers, FHA, VA, USDA, CONV. For appointment call. Hours 830A-5PM

Contact Information

Web Address
https://nrlmortgage.com/

Telephone # 909-821-1305

Camp Verde Business-Downtown

Old World Guns

567 S. Main St. Camp Verde
Family owned and operated antique, collectible
and military surplus firearms. Works with estates
and those with unusual firearms or related pieces.
Tue-Fri 11A-530P, Sat 12P-4P. Call for
appointment.
Contact Information
Web Address
https://www.oldworldgunsllc3.com/
Face Book URL
https://www.facebook.com/oldworldugns
Email: pjonas2@msn.com
Telephone # 928-567-8666   928-202-6899

____

Pete Clark Auto Repair

712 Monte Verde Lane
Honest and Fair. 9A-5P Mon-Fri
Contact Information
Telephone # 928-254-1819

____

PJ Carson Acoustic Music

Acoustic Music including Rock, Country folk,
Jazz and Blues. Serving Camp Verde, Sedona,
Prescott, Cottonwood, Flagstaff and Phoenix.
Contact Information
Telephone # 602-793-4205

____

Raul'S Hair Salon LLC

434 Main Street Ste 4
Camp Verde, AZ 86322
Contact Information
Web Address
http://salonphdaz.com/
Face Book URL
https://www.facebook.com/raulshairsalon
Email: salonphdaz@gmail.com
Telephone # 928-567-9178

____

Razor's Edge Hair Salon

564 S Main Street 109, Camp Verde, AZ 86322
Contact Information
Telephone # 928-567-3227

Saint Vincent De Paul

781 E. Cliffs Pkway
Social & Human Services Organizations,
Religious Organizations.
Contact Information
Web Address
https://ssvpusa.org/
Telephone # 928-567-9471

____

Solid Rock Tile

651 Monte Verde Lane, Camp Verde AZ 86322
Specializing in custom granite and quartz.
Contact Information
Web Address
https://www.solidrocktile.com/
Face Book URL
https://www.facebook.com/Solid-Rock-
Granite-123046537751526/
Email: solidrocktile@aol.com
Telephone # 928-301-1133

____

Camp Verde Business-Downtown

Select Net Autos

675 S Main St, Camp Verde, AZ 86322
We are a small family owned dealership
in Camp Verde, Arizona. Located on Main
Street, we pride ourselves on quality used
vehicles, great prices & service.

Contact Information
Web Address
http://www.selectnetautos.com/
Face Book URL
https://www.facebook.com/Select-Net-Autos-
LLC-331319447287909/about/?ref=page_
internal
Email: selectnetautos@gmail.com
Telephone # 928-254-1362

Salon PhD Professional Hair Designers LLC

590 S Nichols St, Camp Verde, AZ 86322
Beauty salon in Camp Verde, Arizona
Contact Information
Email: Not Available
Telephone # 928-567-9178

Style Up Salon

493 S. Main Street, Camp Verde AZ 86322
Haircuts, Hair Color, foils, all-over color,
Men's barbering, face waxing. 9A-5P Mon-
Friday. Call for an appointment
Contact Information
Face Book URL
https://www.facebook.com/Style-Up-
Salon-420222384699074/
Telephone # 928-567-6788

Taylor and Huntley Financial Group

51 West Hollamon Street, Camp Verde, AZ 86322
Taylor & Huntley Financial Group offers
comprehensive financial planning and wealth
management with offices in Camp Verde,
Cottonwood, and Flagstaff Arizona.
9A-5P Mon-Friday.
Contact Information
Web Address
https://www.thfinancialgroup.com/
Telephone # 928-567-9512

Thanks A Latte

348 Main St. Camp Verde
Sandwiches, coffee
7A-230P Wed- Sunday
Open for Take-Out, dine-in, outside seating
available
Contact Information
Face Book URL
https://www.facebook.com/ThanksALatteCV/
Telephone # 928-567-6450

The Happy Place

Registered Bemer Dealer Nancy Baskerville
698 S. Park Cir.
Experiencing 8 minute sessions with the BEMER
enhances the following: General Blood Flow,
Body's nutrient and Oxygen Supply, Cardiac
Function, Physical Fitness, Endurance, Strength
and Energy, Mental Acuity, Stress Reduction &
Relaxation, Sleep Management, Developed in
Germany, Swiss manufactured. FDA Registered
Medical Device Class 1 and 2.
Contact Information
Email: njbaskerville72@gmail.com

Thompson Paralegal Services

Mailing: PO Box 4681, Camp Verde AZ 86322
348 S. Main, Camp Verde AZ 86322
Legal document preparation, mobile notary, deeds, wills, trusts, business forms, LLC's, divorce, child support. Call for an appointment.

Contact Information

Web Address
https://thompsonlegaldocs.com/
Telephone # 928-300-3013

Top Shelf Liquors and Archery

736 South Main St.
Top of the line bows and hunting supplies. Drive through beer, wine, and liquor.
Hours: Sun-Thurs 9A-830P, Fri, Sat 9A-9P

Contact Information

Face Book URL
https://www.facebook.com/pages/Top-Shelf-Liquors-Archery/1967841203452379/
Telephone # 928-567-6936

√ U Sell It Car Lot

77 General Crook Trail, Camp Verde AZ 86322
Remember the good ol' days when you could shop or sell a vehicle in the Bashas parking lot? We've got you covered! Same set-up, new location at 77 General Crook Trail in the parking lot of New Life Thrift & Gift. As a REOPENING AMERICA SPECIAL, we invite you to park, mark your registration COD, and pay when it sells. No risk!

Contact Information

Telephone # 928-202-9402

Udderly Divine

545 Main St. Camp Verde
Sandwiches, pie, ice cream
7A-5P Closed Sundays
Open for Take-Out, dine-in, outside seating available.

Contact Information

Face Book URL
https://www.facebook.com/udderlydivine/
Telephone # 928-607-0967

Valley Accounting

1st St. , Camp Verde AZ 86322
Tax preparation, payroll services, full-service accounting. You can be sure that our business accountants are knowledgeable and experienced in all areas to help you in the most effective manner. Our business accountants provide the best service to our clients because of their dedication to always doing what is right.

Contact Information

Web Address
https://vvalleyaccounting.com/
Email: ronda@valleyacc.com
Telephone # 928-567-3303

Valley Of The Gun Firearms

515 Highline Lane, Camp Verde, AZ 86322
Class III Sales & Service, $75 NFA Transfers
10% Consignment Sales, $15 FFL Transfers
+ $5 EA Additional, First Responder Supply,
Special Order Items, Firearms Service,
Accessories, Flexible Hours of Operation
We Accept Credit Cards (Additional Fees Apply)

Contact Information

Web Address
https://www.valleyofthegunfirearms.com/
Face Book URL
https://www.facebook.com/valleyofthegunfirearms
Email: valleyofthegunfirearms@yahoo.com
Telephone # 928-925-6631

Camp Verde Business-Downtown

Verde Ditch

432 S. 1st., Camp Verde AZ 86322
Mail: P.O. Box 2345, Camp Verde AZ 86322
Community service/non-profit manages Verde Ditch.

Contact Information

Web Address
https://www.verdeditch.com/links.html
E-Mail
email: verdeditch@yahoo.com
Telephone # 928-567-4212

____

HERE ARE SOME HELPFUL WATER LINKS:

ONLINE CONVERSION: A handy site to convert water measurements.
Web Address
https://www.onlineconversion.com/

Arizona Cooperative Extension:
Providing timely and local science-based information to help Arizona agricultural producers, landowners, businesses, and homeowners produce an abundant and safe food supply, improve their bottom line, and sustain our natural resources.
Web Address
https://extension.arizona.edu/
ADWR: Learn more about water rights in the State of Arizona
Web Address
https://new.azwater.gov/

____

√ Verde Massage

434 S. Main Ste #2, Camp Verde AZ 86322
Caleb Davison Massage Therapist works with muscular, skeletal dysfunctions, deep tissue massage, hot stones, sports, reflexology, cranial-sacral therapy, lymphatic drainage therapy.
 M-Sat 9A-8P, Closed Sunday.

Contact Information

Web Address
https://verdemassage.com/
Face Book URL
https://www.facebook.com/verdemassage/
Email: caleb@verdemassage.com
Telephone # 928-239-5502

____

√ Verde Valley Archaeology Center

460 Finnie Flat Rd., Camp Verde AZ 86322
Museum showcasing regional archaeological heritage with artifact exhibits & a hands-on kids' area. Regular hours 10A-4P Tues-Sat. Please check our website for newest information.

Contact Information

Web Address
https://www.verdevalleyarchaeology.org/
Face Book URL
https://www.facebook.com/
verdevalleyarchaeologycenter/
Email: center@verdevalleyarchaeology.org
Telephone # 928-567-0066

____

Camp Verde Business-Downtown

Verde Valley Resale

348 S. Main St., Camp Verde AZ 86322
Huge vendor mall for arts and crafts, vintage,
antiques, jewelry, furniture.
Contact Information
Face Book URL
https://www.facebook.com/verdevalleyresale/
Telephone # 928-300-5055

____

√ Verde Valley Sanctuary

497 Main St., Camp Verde AZ 86322
Twice Nice Thrift Store with locations in
Cottonwood, Sedona and Camp Verde.
The Verde Valley Sanctuary began in 1993 as
a grassroots organization of women who were
concerned about domestic violence in our
community. The original group of volunteers
began taking crisis calls in their homes and
transporting victims of abuse to the nearest
shelters in Flagstaff, Prescott, and Phoenix. Since
then the Verde Valley Sanctuary has strategically
expanded and now offers comprehensive services
for victims of family violence and assault
including a 28 bed shelter, 24-hour crisis hotline,
advocacy and counseling services, legal support
and community wide education and prevention
programs.
24 Hour Hotline: 800-930-7233
Main Office Telephone: 928 -634-2511 Fax: (928)
Thrift Store open in Camp Verde Tues -Sat 10-
5pm
Contact Information
Web Address
https://verdevalleysanctuary.org/shopping/
Face Book URL
https://www.facebook.com/VerdeValleySanctuary
Telephone # 928-567-8571

Additional Contacts with Verde Valley
Sanctuary
Executive Director: Nicole Florisi
(928) 634-2511

Business Office: Kristel Grace
(928) 634-2511

Education/Prevention: Jennie Underwood
(928) 634-2511

Legal Advocacy Department: Jennie Underwood
(928) 639-2079

Community Development Consultant: Tracey
McConnell
(928) 282-2755

Outreach Director: Jennie Underwood
(928) 634-6255

Shelter Director: Peg Trulson
(928) 634-2511

Twice Nice Sedona: Barry Maketansky
(928) 282-2563

Twice Nice Cottonwood: Matt Meili-Petzoldt
(928) 634-7555

Twice Nice Camp Verde: Jenny Dominique
(928) 567-8571

____

Reserved add space for Chamber adds.

Call to reserve space. Must be a member.

1/4 Page $100, 1/2 Page $200, Full Page $400

Westcott Funeral Home

631 S. St., Camp Verde AZ 86322
Serving families in Camp Verde, Cottonwood and surrounding areas with love, compassion, dignity and respect. Burial Packages, cremation packages, professional services, embalming. See the web site for a complete list of services.

Contact Information

Web Address
https://www.westcottfuneralhome.com/
Telephone # 928-567-3580

Wingfield Bread Company

564 S. Main St., Camp Verde AZ 86322
Freshly milled hand-crafted Artisan breads Sourdough breads, Pastry, Sandwich, Quiche, Salad, Coffee, Tea Pizza. Rachelle Tozza is the great-great granddaughter of original pioneer Wingfield. They grind their own wheat and use fresh ingredients selling at local farmer's markets and out of the plaza. Recently they moved to the Main Street location expanding from loaf bread sales to include a sandwich shop.

Contact Information

Face Book URL
https://www.facebook.com/Wingfield-Bread-Company-284542238384684/
Email: wingfieldbreadco@gmail.com
Telephone # 928-301-9300

√ Yavapai Title Agency

527 S. Main St. Camp Verde AZ 86322
Whether you are a buyer, seller, real estate agent, or lender, we are here to help your real estate needs. Call for an appointment.

Contact Information

Web Address
https://www.yavapaititle.com/
Face Book URL
https://www.facebook.com/yavapaititleagency
Telephone # 928-567-0590

→Finnie Flat

AZ Fire Sprinkler

400 Finnie Flat Rd. #1D. Camp Verde AZ 86322
Home and commercial

Contact Information

Telephone # 928-301-7761 928-567-2243

Alfonsos

452 W Finnie Flat Rd. Suite E
 Mexican Food
Take-out Drive Through Open 24 hr

Contact Information

Web Address
https://alfonsoscampverdeaz.com/
Face Book URL
https://www.facebook.com/pages/Alfonso's%20Mexican%20Food/978636698865523/
Email: familialuna1991@gmail.com
Telephone # 928-567-7296

AutoZone Auto Parts Store #6037

992 West Finnie Flat Rd., Camp Verde AZ 86322
Auto parts store with free check engine light service, tool loaning and rewards program.

Contact Information

Web Address
https://www.autozone.com/locations/az/camp-verde/992-west-finnie-flat-rd.l?cmpid=LOC:US:EN:AD:NL:1000000:GEN:6037
Telephone # 928-325-6145

Camp Verde Business-Finnie Flat

Bashas'

650 W. Finnie Flat Road. Camp Verde AZ 86322
Grocery Store.
Instacart Delivery, Natural Choice Department,
Starbucks. M-Sat: 6A-10P. Sunday 6A-9P.

Contact Information

Web Address
https://www.bashas.com/

Web Address
https://www.bashas.com/stores/bashas-supermarket-hwy-260-finney-flat/

Telephone # 928-567-4585

Bodyworks Massage

452 Finnie Flat Rd, Camp Verde Az 86322

Massages Whether you need to have a moment
of relaxation, reduce muscle tension or attain
relief from chronic pain, a therapeutic massage
can enhance your overall sense of emotional and
physical well-being. Massage therapy can be an
important part of your health maintenance plan
by reducing muscular tension and inflammation
comforting the mind body and soul.

Contact Information

Web Address
https://bodyworksmassagespa.com/

Telephone # 928-351-4880

Camp Verde Eye Care

452 Finnie Flat Rd. Ste 1A, Camp Verde AZ 86322
Dr. Jorge D. Huston OD
We are accepting new patients. Dr. Huston offers
full comprehensive eye exams. We have a full
optical dispensary with over 600 frames to choose
from. Eye exams, glasses, contacts.
M-F 8A-5P (closed 12:00-1:00 for lunch)

Contact Information

Web Address
https://www.cv-eyecare.com/

Telephone # 928-567-3330

Camp Verde Medical Center

1050 Finnie Flat Rd., Camp Verde AZ 86322
Northern Arizona Health Care
On-Site Immediate Care is a walk-in service,
no need to call ahead, where our providers treat
the same conditions treated at urgent care, but
at a lower cost. Patients pay the same co-pay for
an Immediate Care visit as they pay to see their
primary care provider, labs, X-ray.
*Call your Dr. prior to coming to the clinic if you
suspect that you have COVID-19.
M-F 7A-8P, Sat, Sun 8A-5P

Contact Information

Web Address
https://www.nahealth.com/northern-arizona-healthcare-medical-group-camp-verde

Telephone # 928-339-5555

Chase Bank

402 Finnie Flat Rd., Camp Verde AZ 86322
Checking accounts, home lending, car buying and
loans, credit cards, wealth management, Business
banking, ATM. M-F 9:30-4:00 Sat 9:30-12:30

Contact Information

Web Address
https://www.chase.com/

Telephone # 928-567-4111

Camp Verde Business-Finnie Flat

Circle K
700 Finnie Flat Rd., Camp Verde AZ 86322
Gas Station and convenience store. Open 24 Hr
Contact Information
Web Address
https://www.circlek.com/
Telephone # 928-567-8861

CVS Drug Store
522 Finnie Flat Rd., Camp Verde AZ 86322
Drug store and pharmacy. M-SAT 9A-9P, SUN
10A-7P
Contact Information
Web Address
https://www.cvs.com/
Telephone # 928-567-2274

Dollar General
1000 W. Finnie Flat Rd., Camp Verde AZ 86322
Discount grocery, cleaning supplies, seasonal
items and toys. 8A-9P Daily
Contact Information
Web Address
https://www.dollargeneral.com/
Telephone # 928-852-7555

Edward Jones Financial
522 Finnie Flat Rd. Ste H. Camp Verde AZ 86322
Financial Advisor, Financial Advisor, retirement,
investment, market news and guidance
M-Th 6:30A-4:00P
Contact Information
Web Address
https://www.edwardjones.com/us-en/
Telephone # 928-567-0821

Family Dollar
633 Finnie Flat Rd., Camp Verde AZ 86322
Discount grocery, cleaning supplies, seasonal
items and toys. M-Sat 8A-8P, Sun 9A-8P
Contact Information
Web Address
https://www.familydollar.com/
Telephone # 928-567-8894

Hanna's Nails
522 W. Finnie Flat, Camp Verde AZ 86322
Acrylic nails, Gels, pedicure, manicure.
Mon-Sat 9A-7P, Sun 11A-5P
Contact Information
Web Address
https://www.groupon.com/biz/camp-verde-az/
hanas-nails
Telephone # 928-567-6563

Los Zpote's
Mailing: 813 Finnie Flat Rd. Camp Verde, AZ
86322
Family Owned Food Truck, Serving All Of
Arizona & The Verde Valley.
If interested on booking event or private
parties please call Carlos Ponce at (928)-
821-8278 for more information
Contact Information
Face Book URL
https://www.facebook.com/Loszpotes/
Email: loszpotes@gmail.com
Telephone # 928-300-0782

Camp Verde Business-Finnie Flat

Maverick

541 Finnie Flat Rd., Camp Verde AZ 86322
Gas Station and convenience store, Propane exchange, Red Box. 5A-10P daily.
Contact Information
Web Address
https://www.maverik.com/
Telephone # 928-567-7373

NAPA Auto Parts

522 Finnie Flat Rd., Camp Verde AZ 86322
Auto parts, tools and accessories
M-F 7A-6P, Sat 8A-4P
Contact Information
Web Address
https://www.napaonline.com/
Telephone # 928-567-3356

√ National Bank of Arizona

563 Finnie Flat Rd. , Camp Verde AZ 86322
Personal and business banking, home loans, refinancing, mobile banking, personal and auto loans, credit cards. Drive Through, ATM Available
M-Th 9A-5P, Fri 9A-6P
Contact Information
Web Address
https://www.nbarizona.com/
Telephone # 928-567-2404
800-497-8168 General Information 8A-8P
888-224-6622 24 Hr account information

O'Reilly Auto Parts

1016 W. Finnie Flat Rd. , Camp Verde AZ 86322
Auto parts, tools and accessories
M-Sat 7:30A-7:30P, Sun 8A-7:30P
Contact Information
Web Address
https://www.oreillyauto.com/
Telephone # 928-202-3627

Snap Fitness

400 Finnie Flat Rd. , Camp Verde AZ 86322
Fitness Center. Snap Fitness Membership: You Get More as a Member
• No Risk - Month-to-Month Memberships
• Always Open and Nearby
• Non-Intimidating, Friendly and Clean Environment
Call us to Take a Tour of Snap Fitness. Staff on Site. Open 24hr.
Contact Information
Web Address
https://www.snapfitness.com/us/gyms/camp-verde-az/
Face Book URL
https://www.facebook.com/CampVerdeSnapFitness/
Telephone # 928-282-7627

Spectrum Health Services

452 W. Finnie Flat Rd. , Camp Verde AZ 86322
Providing same day services for primary care, behavioral health, pediatrics, and psychiatry. Virtual visits.

Contact Information

Web Address
https://www.spectrumhealthcare-group.com/
Face Book URL
https://www.facebook.com/
SpectrumHealthcareGroup/
EMail: info@SpectrumHealthcare-Group.org
Telephone # 928-567-4026
928-634-2236 Behavioral Health Crisis Line
877-634-7333 CRISIS LINE
928-203-7119 RESPONDER 1ST

____

Starbucks (Bashas)

650 W. Finnie Flat Road
Coffee, pastries
Hours according to Bashes
Take Out, Eat-In

Contact Information

Web Address
https://www.starbucks.com/
Telephone # 928-567-4585

____

√ State Farm Insurance

400 Finnie Flat Rd. #2, , Camp Verde AZ 86322
Karen Cole. State Farm Agent for auto, business, home, property, life, health. Open 8:30-5:00 pm M-F.

Contact Information

Web Address
https://www.kcoleinsurance.com/
Telephone # 928-567-3374

√ Stitches-Steigman Embroidery

452 W Finnie Flat Rd Ste A-2., Camp Verde AZ 86322
Sewing Machine Sales and Repairs. Fabric for Sale, custom embroidery, custom machine quilting, sublimation printing, scissors sharpening service.
Stitches (Formerly Steigman Embroidery) is your one stop shop for sewing machine sales and repairs. Dan is certified in Janome and Bernina repairs and has acquired his Janome Dealership. He also has become an authorized dealer for Nolting Long-Arm machines!
Sewing machines are usually repaired within a day or two. Pricing is listed on our Sewing Machine and Repair page. Please come in and drop off you machine for it's annual service M-F, 9-4.
Monday -Friday 9A-4P Saturday 9A-2P

Contact Information

Web Address
https://stitchescv.com/
Telephone # 928-567-7183

____

Camp Verde Business-Finnie Flat

Tammie's Bread

340 S Groseta Dr, Camp Verde, AZ 86322
Tammie's Bread can be purchased at Ruby Roads
Antique Mall and Camp Verde Farmer's Market
in season. Tammie's Bread bakes breads, pies &
specialty breads fresh the day you want them. Your
not limited by the menu, if you want something
ask. The prices are modest to fit your budget.
Curbside Pick-up.

Contact Information

Face Book URL

https://www.facebook.com/breadwithyouinmind
Email: tammiesbread@gmail.com
Telephone # 928-254-9053

____

The UPS Store

522 Finnie Flat Rd. Camp Verde AZ 86322
Mailbox rental, mailing packages, FAX, scan,
notary service, and copies. M-F 8A-6:30, Sat 9A-
3P

Contact Information

Web Address

https://locations.theupsstore.com/index.html
Telephone # 928-567-7701

____

Tierra Verde Builders

400 Finnie Flat Road, Camp Verde AZ 86322
Mailing Address (P.O. Box 2898, Camp Verde)
Our professional crew is highly qualified and
experienced in all facets of construction
To ensure the safety and quality of your project
we have established, long-term relationships with
subcontractors that are all licensed, bonded and
insured, Design services are available, References
are available. Tierra Verde Builders desires to
assist you in any building project with the utmost
care and concern for all aspects and details that are
important to you. By Appointment.

Contact Information

Web Address

https://www.tierraverdebuilders.com/
Email: info@tierraverdebuilders.com
Telephone # 928-567-2477

____

Tire Pro Automotive

671 Finnie Flat Rd. , Camp Verde AZ 86322
New tires, pressure checks, flats, tire repair, tire
rotation. M-F 7:30A-5, Sat 8A-12P

Contact Information

Web Address

www.tireproautomotive.com
Telephone # 928-567-6339

____

Trader's Corner

813 Finnie Flat Rd. , Camp Verde AZ 86322
Antiques, collectible sales, local honey, Saturday
Flea Market in their parking lot on Finnie Flat.
Tues-Sun 8A-5P

Contact Information

Face Book URL

https://www.facebook.com/Traders-
Corner-335320923334472/
Telephone # 928-567-8745

Camp Verde Business-Finnie Flat

Trails End RV Park

Address:983 Finnie Flat Rd
Camp Verde, AZ 86322
RV Park, dump, propane. Mon: 9:00 AM – 2:00
PM. Tue: 9:00 AM – 2:00 PM, Wed & Sat:9:00 –
11:00 AM, Thu & Fri:9:00 AM – 2:00 PM, Sun:
Closed
Contact Information
Web Address
https://trailsendrvpark.business.site/?utm_
source=gmb&utm_medium=referral
Telephone # 928-240-4897

United Christian School

903 Finnie Flat Rd. Camp Verde AZ 86322
K-8th Grade with Pre-school and summer
programs. Christ centered education and good
academics and small class sizes, kind and caring
teachers, service oriented and happy students.
Contact Information
Web Address
https://www.cvucs.org/
Face Book URL
https://www.facebook.com/United-Christian-
School-Camp-Verde-2078496025778931
Email: office@cvucs.org
Telephone # 928-567-0415

Verde Smiles

430 W Finnie Flat. Ste 107, Camp Verde AZ
86322
Dr. Farad Sharifi
Cosmetic implants, dentures, general dentistry,
Invisalign, restoration, whiting. M-F 8:30-4:30,
Sat by appointment
Contact Information
Web Address
https://verdesmiles.com/
Telephone # 928-567-3799

Walgreens Drug Store

475 W. Finnie Flat Rd. Camp Verde AZ 86322
Drug store and pharmacy. 8A-8P Daily
Contact Information
Web Address
https://www.walgreens.com/
Telephone # 928-239-3187

→Montezuma Highway

Airpower Accessories

884 N. Trails End, Camp Verde Az 86322
Airpower closed its aircraft maintenance
operations at Falcon Field on 12/31/14 and moved
Airpower Accessories to Camp Verde, AZ . We
continue to provide 500 Hour and Overhaul
Services on Starters, Generators, Alternators,
Magnetos and Dry Vacuum Pumps.
Contact Information
Web Address
http://www.airpoweraccessories.com/
Telephone # 928-567-7349

Camp Verde Business-Montezuma Hwy

All in the Polish

155 S. Montezuma Castle Hwy. #5, Camp Verde
AZ 86322
9A-5P Mon-Thurs
Detailing, ceramic coating, paint correction for
autos (and jets). Call for an appointment.
Contact Information
Web Address
https://allinthepolish.com/
Face Book URL
https://www.facebook.com/allinthepolishdetailing
Email: robf@allinthepolish.com
Telephone # 928-352-3537, 928-634-2580

———————

Always a Kid at Heart

AZ Pops by Janet Walther
Mobil Popsicle Stand in Camp Verde
Gourmet Popsicles. Free delivery to your door
Verde Valley and Sedona. 12 flavors to mix
and match, 3 flavors are just fruited no added
sweeteners. Healthy fruit puree or chocolate
flavors that are very flavorful and not like what
you buy in the stores. No dyes, no preservatives,
65% AZ fruit. Each popsicle is individually sealed
with flavor and ingredient list on the front. Call
or email for a current list of flavors. Qty of 10
Gourmet Popsicles in a pack perfect for gifts
for Father's Day, Birthdays or Birthday Parties,
employees, mood booster for friends or yourself.
Free delivery, Gift message available.
Contact Information
Email: janet_walther@yahoo.com
Telephone # 760-271-8506

———————

Babe's Round Up

90 S. Montezuma Castle Hwy.
Mon-Sat 11A-9P Closed Sunday
Local BBQ. Pulled Pork, beef brisket, BBQ chicken
with cowboy beans. Look for the smoker out
front. Walk up window, Take Out, dine-in, outside
seating.
Contact Information
Telephone # 928-567-6969
For catering 928-821-0205

———————

Beto's Corner

10 E. Cliff House Drive
7A-8P Mon-Fri 7A-2P Saturday. Closed Sunday
Take-out, drive-through window, eat-in
Contact Information
Web Address Recommendation
https://betoscorner.food62.com/
Face Book URL
https://www.facebook.com/pages/Beto's%20
Corner/109385769099709/
Telephone # 928-567-8897

———————

√ Camp Verde Community Library

Friends of Camp Verde Library
130 Black Bridge Rd. Camp Verde AZ 86322
Kid and family, teens and adult programs, classes,
free use of rooms, free use of computers and lots
of books. Offers summer programs for children
in conjunction with Camp Verde Parks and
Recreation.
M-Th 9:00-8P, Fri-Sat 9A-5P, Closed Sunday.
Contact Information
Web Address
https://www.campverde.az.gov/departments/
community-library
Face Book URL
https://www.facebook.com/campverdelibrary/
Email: library@campverde.az.gov
Telephone # 928-554-8380

Camp Verde Mini and RV Storage

60 N Montezuma Castle Hwy, Camp Verde
Call or email us for availability Storage is open
24/7 with electronic gate access! All rentals are
month to month.

Contact Information

Web Address
https://campverdeministorage.com/
Email: info@campverdeministorage.com
Telephone # 928-567-6840

———————

Central AZ Sports and Physical Therapy

155 S. Montezuma Castle Hwy. Suite 2
Camp Verde, Az. 86322
We are a small independently Owned and operated
Physical Therapy Clinic. We accept Most most
major insurance as well as Worker Comp Auto
accident claims and Triwest for our Veterans. We
pride our selves on our friendly staff and clinic
atmosphere and work very hard to meet the needs
of Each and everyone of our patients. PTA is
Miss Sherry Houser as well as our volunteer Miss
Ryliee Smith. Our hours of operation are Monday
through Friday 7:00 am to 3:30 pm if you have any
questions please give us a call here at the Clinic
Dave Castillo or Myself Cherie Battise will help
you in any way we can.

Contact Information

Face Book URL
https://www.facebook.com/cazspt/
Email: email: cazspt@gmail.com
Telephone # 928-300-1936 (office)
928-567-8826 (FAX)

———————

Fit-In-15

155 S Montezuma Castle Highway Suite 7, Camp
Verde AZ 86322
Personal training, fitness therapy, senior fitness,
and performance nutrition.

Contact Information

Face Book URL
https://www.facebook.com/dickandlisa/
Email: dicknunez@aol.com
Telephone # 928-567-3262

———————

Franklin Pest Control

Address: 1362 N Powderhorn Rd. Camp Verde,
AZ 86322
Franklin Pest Control specializes in pest control
services for residential, commercial and real
estate properties for Northern and Central
Arizona.

Contact Information

Face Book URL
https://www.facebook.com/FrankinPestControl/
Telephone # 928-202-6915

———————

Hauser & Hauser Farms

652 Montezuma Castle Hwy. Camp Verde AZ
86322
Alpha and wheat sales. Fresh sweet corn roadside
stands in summertime and early fall. Corn sales
are happening! Check out the Hauser Family
Cookbook on Amazon.

Contact Information

Web Address
https://www.hauserandhauserfarms.com/
Face Book URL
https://www.facebook.com/Hauser-and-Hauser-
Farms-434461259981906
Email: hauserfarms@aol.com
Telephone # 928-567-2142

Camp Verde Business-Montezuma Hwy

Hauser Family Cook Book

Some years back, Brenda Hauser, armed with a tin box, an old wood table, a folding chair and an umbrella, set up at the two-acre sweet corn patch on their property. Corn sold for fifty cents a dozen. She says that it was fun to see people come down the dusty road in their clean white cars and high heels to pick corn. It was such a success that the next year they planted five acres. They released the family cookbook in 2020. It is a local tradition filled with corn recipes. **Amazon Link** to order a Hauser Family Cookbook: https://www.amazon.com/Hauser-Family-Cookbook-Kristi-Bright/dp/B08GFPM85G/

____

Home Smart Elite

1841 N. Montezuma Hts. Rd. Camp Verde, AZ 86322
Brenda Powell
Contact Information
E-Mail
email: ranchoverderealestate@gmail.com
Telephone # 928-301-3665

____

Kilby & Sons Construction

282 E Zellner Ln. Camp Verde, AZ 86322
Construction
Contact Information
Telephone # 928-300-9481

Krazy K RV Park

2075 Arena Del Loma, Camp Verde, AZ 86322
Welcome to the Krazy K RV Park. Located in historic Verde Valley. Close to Montezuma Castle, Sedona, Jerome, Fort Verde State Park, We have a Pool, Hot Tub (seasonal). Laundry, Clean Rest Rooms with Showers, Free WiFi at WiFi Station, Exercise Room, We are pet friendly, However we don't allow dog pens.
Contact Information
Web Address
https://krazykrv.com/
Face Book URL
https://www.facebook.com/pages/Krazy%20Krv%20Park/170091866334372/
Telephone # 928-567-0565

____

LC Studio Hair and Nails

155 S. Montezuma Castle Hwy #4, Camp Verde, AZ 86322
Call for an appointment.
Contact Information
Telephone #
Hair by Cindy 928-224-2626
Nails by Latahna 928-275-7228

____

Love Yourself Love Your Health

155 S. Montezuma Castle Hwy #3 Camp Verde, AZ 86322
Lisa Diacik. Call for an appointment
Contact Information
Telephone # 928-399-6299

Reserved add space for Chamber adds.

Call to reserve space. Must be a member.

1/4 Page $100, 1/2 Page $200, Full Page $400

Camp Verde Business-Montezuma Hwy

Majestic Flooring LLC

155 S. Montezuma Castle Hwy. Camp Verde, AZ 86322

Custom wood flooring, engineered laminate, luxury vinyl, tile, carpet, counter tops, quartz, granite. Call for an appointment.

Contact Information

Web Address

http://www.azmajesticflooring.com/

Email: azmajesticflooring@gmail.com

Telephone #

Poppy Walls 928-215-6164

Jacob Miller 714-904-6211

———————

Montezuma Realty

115 S. Montezuma Castle Hwy. Camp Verde, AZ 86322

Pete Roulette Real Estate Broker. Agent for New Manufactured Homes. Montezuma Realty is a small business that is locally owned and operated. Our Realtors have had the privilege of serving Camp Verde for more than 20 years.

Contact Information

Web Address

https://visitcampverde.com/campverde/montezuma-realty

Face Book URL

https://www.facebook.com/Misty-Weatherford-Montezuma-Realty-1002827315478055/

Telephone # 928-567-4599 928-567-4318

———————

Mower Medic LLC

475 W Mesa Ln, Camp Verde, AZ 86322

Contact Information

Web Address

https://mower-medic-llc.business.site/

Email: None Available

Telephone # 928-567-8661

Noguez Farm

87 W. Charolais Dr. Camp Verde AZ, 86322

Farm fresh produce locally grown pesticide free open daily in the summer time 8:00am - 5:00 pm Selling tomatoes, okra, cucumbers, green onions, garlic, roasted chilies, squash, green beans, black eyed peas, melons.

Contact Information

Face Book URL

https://www.facebook.com/Noguez-Farm-1078955318873076/?ref=page_internal

Email: None Available

Telephone # None Available

———————

√ Phillip England Center for the Performing Arts Foundation

210 Camp Lincoln Road, Camp Verde, AZ 86322

Mailing: 385 S. Main St. Camp Verde, AZ 86322

A live music venue for jazz, blues, country and classical. We are committed to being the premier theater for cultural, educational and artistic expression for the Sedona and Verde Valley area.

Contact Information

Web Address

https://www.pecpaf.org/

Face Book URL

https://www.facebook.com/pecpaf

Email: pecpaf@pecpaf.com

———————

Camp Verde Business-Middle Verde Rd

Rays Of Sunshine Center Inc

30 Cliffhouse Dr. Camp Verde, AZ 86322
Welcome to rays of sunshine child care center!
Rays has been taking care of little ones for
more than 10 years! Rays is state certified, state
inspected, and fully insured to provide the best
care for your children. Rays has access to several
state programs that can assist with child care costs
for those who need assistance and rays provides
daily meals as well!

Rays provides both pre-school and child care
services. Your child will be inspired, entertained,
have loads of fun and be learning all at the same
time! Give us a call to arrange a tour of rays and
see for yourself.

Contact Information

Web Address
http://raysofsunshinechildcarecenter.com/
Face Book URL
https://www.facebook.com/raysofsunshineofficial
Email: raysofsunshine2@outlook.com
Telephone # 928-567-6299

Renovare Wellness Center

155 S. Montezuma Castle Hwy #3, Camp Verde
AZ, 86322
Energy work, nutritional counseling, infrared
sauna. Call for appointment.

Contact Information

Telephone # 928-202-0538

Sonic

350 Castle Lane
Fast Food, burger, Ice cream
Take-out, drive-in window, Dine-In

Contact Information

Web Address
https://www.sonicdrivein.com/
Face Book URL
https://www.facebook.com/sonicdrivein
Telephone # 928-567-7062

→Middle Verde Rd

Advanced Cleaning Technologies

555 W Mesa Ln., Camp Verde, AZ 86322
Carpet Cleaning, Chimney Sweeps, Air Duct
Cleaning, Tile & Grout Cleaning. Service Area:
Flagstaff, Prescott, Sedona, Payson, Prescott
Valley, Happy Jack, Williams, Grand Canyon,
Humboldt, Tuba City, Gray Mountain, Congress,
Cottonwood, Fredonia, Kirkland, Parks, North
Rim, Pine, Mormon Lake, Munds Park, Chino
Valley, Flag Staff, Paulden

At Advanced Cleaning Technologies A-Z, we
believe in up-front pricing with no pushy sales
people and no games. This ensures that you
receive the best carpet cleaning solutions at the
best prices. Please call today for more information,
and be sure to ask about our free carpet
evaluations.

Contact Information

Web Address
https://www.cleaningaz.com/
Face Book URL
https://www.facebook.com/
Advancedcleaningtechnologies/?_rdc=2&_rdr
Email: advancedcleaningtechnologies@msn.com
Telephone # 928-300-7452

Camp Verde Business-Middle Verde Rd

Alfredo's Wife

3210 N. Lost River Dr, Camp Verde AZ 86322
Our mission is to create comfortable, casual, resort and cruise wear artfully adorned with whimsical and colorful appliques' including jewel and stud embellishments. Simple designs, elegant colors and natural fabrics these are the trademark qualities that make Ava Dering's clothing line special and unique. Check out our current designs by clicking on "Clothing Gallery" and/or "What's New" We're always adding new things, so check back often!

Contact Information
Web Address
http://www.alfredoswife.com/
Face Book URL
https://www.facebook.com/alfredoswife/
Telephone # 928-634-8616

Alternative Choices

2436 N. Lagrande Dr. W,
Camp Verde Az 86322
We strive to create a society that is more inclusive of all individuals. We seek to build trust, understanding and acceptance within our local communities through interaction, active participation and experience. Our mission is to help all individuals live independent, productive lives. It is the goal of Alternative Choices to build on an individual's skills and abilities through positive encouragement, guided repetition and following their Person-Centered Plan so that they can be successful in their community.

Contact Information
Web Address
http://www.choosecra.com/
Face Book URL
www.facebook.com/A-choices.com
Telephone # 928-639-4574

Chevron Gas Station & Market Place

320 Castle Lane
Gas, ATM, Arizona Lottery, Ice, Snacks, firewood.
Open 24 hr
Contact Information
Web Address
https://www.yan-whitehills.com/
Telephone # 928-554-7031

√ Cliff Castle Casino Hotel

Located in Cliff Castle Casino Hotel
555 W Middle Verde Rd
Casino and Hotel, live entertainment, shows, meetings, and weddings. With 122 well-appointed rooms, the Tower is the first six-story hotel in the Verde Valley.

Contact Information
Web Address
https://www.cliffcastlecasinohotel.com/
Face Book URL
https://www.facebook.com/CliffCastleCasino
Email: guestservices@cliffcastlecasinohotel.com
Telephone # 1-800-381-7568 928-567-7999

Cliff Dwellers Bar

Located in Cliff Castle Casino Hotel
555 W Middle Verde Rd
As though carved into high cliff walls, this unique bar offers great vantage points for you to watch live entertainment at Dragonfly Lounge and the excitement of the casino floor.

Contact Information
Web Address
https://www.cliffcastlecasinohotel.com/
Face Book URL
https://www.facebook.com/CliffCastleCasino
Email: guestservices@cliffcastlecasinohotel.com
Telephone # 1-800-381-7568 928-567-7999

Camp Verde Business-Middle Verde Rd

Creative Dental Designs

2170 N Mooney Ln, Camp Verde, AZ 86322
Creative Dental Designs has 34 years of experience serving dentists with all of their crown and bridge needs. We specialize in all ceramic restorations, full contour Zirconia crowns and bridges designed and milled on premises. ORIGIN® Beyond™ high translucency zirconia, hand stacked Zirconia porcelain fused to Zirconia frames and beautiful porcelain laminates. For those with more traditional tastes we offer all aspects of porcelain fused to metal and full gold crowns and bridges are available. We pride ourselves in quality work and unsurpassed service with all of our clients. Join us for a hassle free lab experience.

Contact Information

Web Address
https://campverdebiz.com/
Face Book URL
http://creativedentaldesigns.com/
Email: support@CreativeDentalDesignsAZ.om
Telephone # 928-282-3082

Custom Xray
Custom X Ray Managed Services

Montezuma-Middle Verde Road
Custom XRay offers full service & repairs for all makes and models of Imaging Equipment, Medical Equipment. Sales - Leasing - Rentals of all types of Imaging Equipment, Medical Equipment, Rehab and Physical Therapy Equipment. Managed Services - we provide construction assistance, lead shielding, architecture drawings for new practices, clinics, hospitals, correctional facilities, mobile x-ray, and equine & small animal practices. Custom XRay offers service, support and sales throughout Arizona and the Southwest Region. Services, Repairs, Support and Sales we are open Monday - Friday with on-call staff for after hours and weekends.

Contact Information

Web Address
https://www.customxray.com/
Telephone # 602-525-0630

Distant Drums RV Resort

582 W. Middle Verde Rd
Pool, Spa, Fitness Center, and Bar. The bus that goes to the Casino. Country store.

Contact Information

Web Address
https://ddrvresort.com/
Face Book URL
https://www.facebook.com/
DistantDrumsRVResort/
Email: info@ddrvresort.com
Telephone # 928-554-8000

Camp Verde Business-Middle Verde Rd

El Dorado Residential Care Home

3363 W. Middle Verde Road

4100 Sq Foot, Assisted living Care home located in the heart of the green-belt in the Verde Valley, Arizona. Fully furnished private and semi-private rooms. 24 hr supervision and assistance. Housekeeping and laundry services. 3 Well balanced nutritious meals and snacks daily. Enhanced daily activities. Assistance with bathing, grooming and dressing.

Contact Information

Face Book URL

https://www.facebook.com/El-Dorado-Residential-Care-Home-145324665580139/

Telephone # 928-567-3304

Ernie's Tobacco Shop

333 W. Middle Verde Road

Great prices on smokes. 8A-6:30 7 days a week

Contact Information

Telephone # 928-567-0014

Fables Bar

Located in Cliff Castle Casino Hotel

555 W Middle Verde Rd

Fables is a great place to relax, watch the game or talk with friends. Located next door to Storytellers, you can enjoy a before-dinner cocktail.

Contact Information

Web Address

https://www.cliffcastlecasinohotel.com/

Face Book URL

https://www.facebook.com/CliffCastleCasino

Email: guestservices@cliffcastlecasinohotel.com

Telephone # 1-800-381-7568   928-567-7999

Jackpot Ranch

2025 Reservation Loop Road

Events, guest lodging, corporate events, weddings and receptions, spiritual and youth retreats.

Contact Information

Web Address

https://jackpotranch.org/

Face Book URL

https://www.facebook.com/jackpotranch

Email: managerjackpotranch@gmail.com

Telephone # 928-300-5490

Johnny Rockets

Located in Cliff Castle Casino Hotel

555 W Middle Verde Rd

Travel back to the '50s for a dining experience loaded with nostalgic charm. Enjoy all-American favorites: cooked-to-order burgers, fries, fresh-baked apple pie, and hand-dipped malts and shakes.

Contact Information

Web Address

https://www.cliffcastlecasinohotel.com/

Face Book URL

https://www.facebook.com/CliffCastleCasino

Email: guestservices@cliffcastlecasinohotel.com

Telephone #

1-800-381-7568 928-567-7999

Camp Verde Business-Middle Verde Rd.

Metropolis Support, LLC

2933 W Middle Verde Road Camp Verde, AZ 86322

VICS would like to introduce "Metropolis Business Accounting" (MBA) is a fully integrated wholesale distribution system with a generic wholesale/distribution interface and specialized interfaces designed specifically for the sportswear distribution industry, veterinary systems, ball bearing wholesalers, cap wholesalers, and many more. We also design specialized interfaces for industries for which there are no off-the-shelf solutions available.

Contact Information

Web Address

http://www.metropolissupport.com/index.html

Email: Cheryl -- cheryl@vicsmba.com

Email: Eric -- flash@vicsmba.com

Telephone # Ph. 928-567-3727

Telephone # Ph. 928-567-3529

FAX # 928-567-6122

Mountain Springs Buffet

Located in Cliff Castle Casino Hotel

555 W Middle Verde Rd

Mountain Springs Buffet offers all of your favorite dishes, in a beautiful setting. Enjoy a sumptuous Sunday Brunch. Buffet prices start at just $8; drinks (non-alcoholic) are included. Hours: 7am – 10pm, Sunday – Thursday, 7am – 11pm, Friday & Saturday

Contact Information

Web Address

https://www.cliffcastlecasinohotel.com/

Face Book URL

https://www.facebook.com/CliffCastleCasino

Email: guestservices@cliffcastlecasinohotel.com

Telephone # 928-567-5158

Mower Medic

475 W Mesa Lane

Camp Verde, AZ 86322

Contact Information

Telephone # 928-274-0239

Rainbow Acres

2120 Reservation Loop Rd.

Rainbow Acres is a Christian community with heart that empowers persons with developmental disabilities to live to their fullest potential with dignity and purpose. We provide exceptional housing, life-enriching programs, and loving, holistic care in a safe, vibrant, inclusive ranch-style community.

Contact Information

Web Address

https://rainbowacres.com/

Face Book URL

https://www.facebook.com/RainbowAcresAZ/

Email: info@rainbowacres.com

Telephone # 928-567-5231

Scott Brothers Drywall

Camp Verde

Drywall Contractors

You tube video: https://www.youtube.com/watch?v=pbG9LxCyfpQ

Contact Information

Email: Not Available

Telephone # 928-554-0110

Camp Verde Business-Middle Verde Rd.

Storytellers
Located in Cliff Castle Casino Hotel
555 W Middle Verde Rd
Fine vintage from the extensive wine list includes local varieties from the local vineyards. Chef de Cuisine Andrea Di Luca creates a menu that tantalizes the taste buds. With its rock walls and gentle waterfall, Storytellers captures the spirit of ancient Indian dwellings. 5pm – 9pm, Wednesday and Thursday 5pm – 10pm, Friday and Saturday, 5pm – 9pm, Sunday, Closed, Monday and Tuesday
Contact Information
Web Address
https://www.cliffcastlecasinohotel.com/
Face Book URL
https://www.facebook.com/CliffCastleCasino
Email: guestservices@cliffcastlecasinohotel.com
Telephone # For reservations call 928-567-7905

____

The Café
Located in Cliff Castle Casino Hotel
555 W Middle Verde Rd
The Café, located in the Hotel portion of Cliff Castle, is open for business and pleasure. Purchase yummy pastries, muffins and coffees to go, or relax in the spacious dining area. Open in AM.
Contact Information
Web Address
https://www.cliffcastlecasinohotel.com/
Face Book URL
https://www.facebook.com/CliffCastleCasino
Email: guestservices@cliffcastlecasinohotel.com
Telephone # 928-567-5158

____

Three Sisters Market
Located in Cliff Castle Casino Hotel
555 W Middle Verde Rd
Need a light meal or snack? No matter what the hour, this 24/7 grab-and-go bistro is the go-to place for gourmet coffee, hot breakfast, made-to-order burgers and sandwiches. Choose from a fine selection of your favorite appetizers, soups and salads.
Contact Information
Web Address
https://www.cliffcastlecasinohotel.com/
Face Book URL
https://www.facebook.com/CliffCastleCasino
Email: guestservices@cliffcastlecasinohotel.com
Telephone # 928-567-5158

____

Waugh Machine
3413 Middle Verde Rd
Camp Verde, AZ 86322
Contact Information
Telephone # 928-567-3066

____

Yavapai Apache Fry Bread and Jewelry
W. Middle Verde Road
Fresh fry bread and Native American Jewelry. Look for the white tent next to Ernie's.
10A-5P Daily

____

→Hwy 260 East of I-17

ABB Etch Co.
783 E. Howards Rd.
1655 S Sullivan Ln, # 1
Industry: Coating, Engraving, and Allied Services,
N.E.C
Contact Information
Telephone # 928-567-9935

____

All American Pet Products Inc

PO Box 687 Camp Verde, AZ
All American Pet Products, Inc. is a family-owned
business, located in Northern Arizona. We are the
largest breeders of Doberman Pinschers in the
country for over 10 years.
Contact Information
Web Address
http://www.breedersselect.com
Web Address
https://www.voofla.com/US/Camp-
Verde/184166191654031/All-American-Pet-
Products
Telephone # 928-567-8459

____

All Pro Motorcycle & ATV Repair
873 East Howard Rd. Ste 16
Full-Service parts & repair. 9A-5P Hours
Contact Information
Email: allpro.uhler@gmail.com
Telephone # 928-567-3183

____

Ameri-Gas
624 N. Industrial Dr.
Propane, residential and business delivery, grill,
and RV cylinders. Grill tank exchange program.
M-F 8A-4P
Contact Information
Web Address
https://www.amerigas.com/
Telephone # 928-567-4099

____

American Steel Carports
Howard Rd. Camp Verde
Authorized Dealer. Arena, barns, garages, sheds,
warehouses.
Contact Information
Web Address
https://www.carportcentral.com/metal-carports-
camp-verde-az
Telephone # 980-217-0441

____

√ Anasazi Animal Clinic
407 W Highway 260
Anasazi Animal Clinic is a full service animal
clinic and will take both emergency cases as
well as less urgent medical, surgical, and dental
issues, boarding and house calls. Dr. Gary Pollock
is experienced in all types of conditions and
treatments. Kid-friendly calm environment. We
can do most blood work in as little as 15 minutes.
With this technology it will enables us to provide
immediate and better care for your pet. We also
offer the best in nutrition, we carry Hill's products,
Science Diet and Prescription Diet foods for dogs
and cats. M-F 8A-5PM
Contact Information
Web Address
http://www.anasazianimalclinic.com/
Face Book URL
https://www.facebook.com/Anasazi-Animal-
Clinic-153485504677488
Email: anasazianimalclinic@gmail.com
Telephone # 928-567-3807

Anchor Cross Ranch

653 W Fir St, Camp Verde Az 86322
Anchor Cross Ranch is a private horse training
and specialized boarding facility located in Camp
Verde, Arizona. Bob Grant specializes in Ranch
Performance Horses, including Working
Cow Horses, Cutting Horses and the ever popular
Ranch Riding and Ranch Trail. These horses
are crossing over successfully into NRCHA and
AQHA Reined Cow Horse competitions, Reined
Cow Horse Herd Work and local Ranch Cutting
classes. He believes that putting a strong basic
foundation on a young horse and keeping it fun
and rewarding is the best approach to finding the
strengths and abilities of each individual horse.
Horses in training are given substantial time turned
out in improved irrigated pastures with compatible
buddies near by, we firmly believe this practice
helps to keep a sane mind and strong body.

Contact Information
Web Address
http://www.anchorcrossranch.com/
Face Book URL
https://www.facebook.com/AnchorCross/
Telephone # 928-853-6179

BAR LH FARMS LLC

Angel 1 Transportation

Camp Verde, AZ
Angel 1 Transportation And Tour from Camp
Verde, AZ. Company specialized in: Tour
Operators. Call us for more
Contact Information
Email: Not Available
Telephone # 928-554-4459

B & B Transmission & Auto

725 E Howards Rd Ste C
Contact Information
Telephone # 928-567-8650

√ Bar LH Farms, LLC

Mailing address; 1686 S. Reeves Arena Rd.

Camp Verde Az, 86322
Raises and sells grain fed, organic beef. We also
have an Airbnb.

Contact Information
Email; barlhfarmsLLC@gmail.com
Telephone # 602-809-1245

√ Betty Sue's Quilting LLC

2040 S. Derby Drive Camp Verde AZ 86322
Specializing in computerized quilting with edge to
edge and custom designs.
Contact Information
Telephone # 623-505-8591

Bobs Tree & Landscape Co

771 Howard Rd.
A complete Tree Service & Landscaping Company
Fire Wood for Sale.
Contact Information
Telephone # 928-567-6744 1-800-564-1688

____

Brady Custom Builders

1825 S Quarterhorse Ln., Camp Verde Az 86322
Brady custom builders is a family owned company
that strives to become the construction company
of your choice now and for all your future
construction needs.ROC # 325575
Contact Information
Web Address
Face Book URL
https://www.facebook.com/bradycustombuilders/
about/
Email: jeremy@bradycustombuilders.com
Telephone # 928-710-8731

____

Bread of Life Missions Inc

873 S. Howard Rd.
Mail: P.O. Box 2991
Non-profit food distribution for those who qualify.
Free food distribution at the warehouse-on call.
Due to current COVID guidelines, Call the # for
the newest food distributions.
Contact Information
Web Address
https://www.breadoflifeaz.org/
Telephone # 928-567-6931

____

Burger King

365 N. Goswick Way
6A-9P Mon-Sat, 7A-9P Sunday
Take-out, Drive Through window
Contact Information
Web Address
https://www.bk.com/
Face Book URL
https://www.facebook.com/burgerking
Telephone # 928-567-3401

____

Canyon Wood Supply

1608 S Murdock Rd, Camp Verde, AZ 86322
Firewood Sales & Delivery
Hours: Mon-Fri 6 AM - 2:30 PM
Contact Information
Face Book URL
https://www.facebook.com/pages/Canyon%20
Wood%20Supply/124988674221507/
Email: Not Available
Telephone # 928-567-3481

____

Camp Verde 24 Hr Storage

603 Industrial Dr
Open daily with gate access to storage units 24 hours a day. Need to access your belongings after work or work a late-night shift? Rent directly On-Line or visit our Kiosk where you can rent on-site or by phone. 24 Hour Surveillance System in Place, Close access to Hwy 17 and SR 260! Call 9285673000 for availability!

Contact Information

Web Address
https://www.campverde24hourstorage.com/
Rent a Storage on Line
https://campverde24hourstorage.
storageunitsoftware.com/pages/rent
Face Book URL
https://www.facebook.com/Camp-Verde-24-Hour-Storage-1044940902313040/
Email: campverde24hourstorage@yahoo.com
Telephone # 928-567-3000

———————

Canyon State Concrete

541 Howard Rd.
Mail: PO Box 1954

Contact Information

Web Address
https://www.allthearizona.com/Local/Arizona/Camp_Verde/Concrete+Contractors/canyon-state-concrete_17042569
Telephone # 9285676786

———————

Clear Creek RV Park

4483 E Hwy 260
Camp Verde, AZ 86322

Contact Information

Face Book URL
https://www.facebook.com/pages/Clear%20Creek%20RV%20Park/104955306213933/
Telephone # 928-300-3705

Clear Creek Vineyard & Winery

4053 Hwy 260
A family-owned vineyard and winery dedicated to producing quality, organic wine. Join us for a glass today! Open this summer Fridays, Saturdays, and Sundays from 11:00 am until 5:00 PM.

Contact Information

Web Address
https://clearcreekwineryaz.com/
Face Book URL
https://www.facebook.com/CCVWRioClaroWines
Email: mesa@clearcreekwineryaz.com
Telephone # 602-859-7418

———————

Comfort Inn Camp Verde

340 N. Goswick Wy.
Pool, Spa, Wifi, free breakfast, business center
24hr front desk
Contact Information

Web Address
https://www.choicehotels.com/
Telephone # 928-567-9000

———————

Copper Canyon Inn

550 Hwy 260
Swimming pool, hot tub. No pets. Free Wifi.

Contact Information

Face Book URL
https://www.facebook.com/coppercanyoninn
Email: coppercanyoninn@gmail.com
Telephone # 928-567-2622

Reserved add space for Chamber adds.

Call to reserve space. Must be a member.

1/4 Page $100, 1/2 Page $200, Full Page $400

Reserved add space for Chamber adds.

Call to reserve space. Must be a member.

1/4 Page $100, 1/2 Page $200, Full Page $400

Camp Verde Business-HWY 260 East of I-17

D-Best Plumbing

801 E. Howard

18 years experience, quality craftsmanship. Install plumbing in new construction. 24 hr emergency service available. Roc Lic 303307CR 37

M-Sat 8A-5P

Contact Information

Web Address

https://www.d-bestplumbing.com/

Face Book URL

https://www.facebook.com/DBestPlumbinginc/about/?ref=page_internal

Email: pettyplumber@gmail.com

Telephone # 928-567-8755

____

Dairy Queen

1580 W. State Route 260

Ice Cream, Fast Food

Drive Through Window, dine-in

Contact Information

Web Address

https://www.dairyqueen.com/en-us/

Face Book URL

https://www.facebook.com/dairyqueen

Telephone # 928-567-3229

____

Days Inn & Suites Camp Verde

1640 SR 260

Plan your getaway to sunny Arizona and book a room at our Days Inn Camp Verde. Located off I-17, our Camp Verde location near Cliff Castle Casino is halfway between Phoenix and Flagstaff. From our hotel, enjoy easy access to the most popular attractions in the area. Enjoy free breakfast and WiFi—plus, a pool. Accessible rooms are available at our non-smoking hotel.

Contact Information

Web Address

https://www.wyndhamhotels.com/days-inn/camp-verde-arizona/days-inn-camp-verde-arizona/overview?CID=LC:DI:20160927:RIO:Local:SM-

dimotn&iata=00093796

Telephone #

Reservations: 844-261-2741

Local # 928-567-3700

____

Denny's

1630 West Arizona Hwy 260

All American Food

You can order ahead at Dennys.com or give us a call at 9285679505

Hours are 7am-10pm. Kids Eat Free 7 Days a week, all day long! 2 kid's meals for every 1 adult entree purchased. Open for dine-in, take out, and curbside pickup.

Contact Information

Web Address

https://www.dennys.com/order

Face Book URL

https://www.facebook.com/dennys/

Telephone # 928-567-9505

____

Dos Tortugas LLC

3300 S. Sierra Ln

Camp Verde, AZ 86322

Contact Information

Face Book URL

https://www.facebook.com/dostortugas2016

Email: dostortugas2016@gmail.com

Telephone # 928-300-7533

____

Eagle Eye Barrels

120 Hwy 260
Open daily 10 to 4 social distancing, air condition showroom, freshly renewed deck and canopy with cooling misters, lots of new inventory and ready for custom orders. We have an amazing Furniture building classes starting soon. Watch for our weekly dates.

Contact Information

Web Address
https://eagleeyebarrel.com/
Face Book URL
https://www.facebook.com/eagleeyebarrels/
Email: eagleeyebarrels@gmail.com
Telephone # 928-821-3089

———————

Energy Roofers

1630 Road Ranger Lane
Mail: P.O. Box 2154
Spray Polyurethane Foam, Commercial, residential, foam roofing, coating and repair. Licensed, Bonded & Insured For Commercial And Residential roofing. We can re-roof. Variety of roof types to choose from Tear Off & Replace Any Roof Replace Entirely with a Metal Roof Serving Northern AZ since 1984! Variety of roof types to choose from. We are the ONLY Roofing Company in Northern AZ offering Polyurethane Foam Roofs! Energy Roofers is a Licensed, Bonded, and Insured Roofing Contractor with the Arizona Registrar of Contractors. AZROC #: 215643

Contact Information

Web Address
https://www.energyroofers.com/
Email: office@energyroofers.com
Telephone # Get a quote: 928-567-3140

———————

Ernies 76 Station

20 E. Hwy 260
Gas and Convenience Store. Fill up and pay using the My 76® App to play Wheel of Destiny.

Contact Information

Web Address
https://www.76.com/
Telephone # 928-567-6270

———————

Filberto's

1650 W. State Route 260
Mexican Food
Drive Through Window Open 24 hr
Eat In dining, Take-out

Contact Information

Web Address
https://filibertos.com/
Face Book URL
https://www.facebook.com/FilibertosMexFood/
Telephone # 928-567-8754

———————

Ferrell Gas

523 N. Industrial Dr.
Propane, residential and business delivery, auto gas refueling station, grill and RV cylinders.
M-F 8A-5P

Contact Information

Web Address
https://www.ferrellgas.com/
Telephone # 928-567-3274

Firebird Towing

573 Industrial Dr. Camp Verde, AZ 86322
Family owned and operated. Open 24/7
including holidays. Serving the Verde Valley and
surrounding areas

Contact Information

Face Book URL
https://www.facebook.com/Firebird-Towing-361865663938864
Telephone # 928-451-5788

√ Flew the Coop Nashville Hot Chicken Shack

1620 AZ-260 Suite D
Buttermilk Brined All-Natural Fried Chicken
Breast dredged in our house dip then sprinkled
with FTC's own spice blend, served on a Butter
Toasted Brioche Bun. Choice of sides and Heat.
Dine in, Take-Out. Open Every Day: 10am – 9pm.

Contact Information

Web Address
https://flewthecoophotchicken.com/
Face Book URL
https://www.facebook.com/
flewthecoophotchicken/
Telephone # (928)238-1422

Gabriela's

1580 W. State Route 260 Ste 2
Mexican Food
Monday - Thursday 7 A-4P, Friday -Sunday 7
A-8P
Drive Through Window & Take out

Contact Information

Web Address
https://www.gabrielasmexicanfood.com/
Face Book URL
https://www.facebook.com/GabrielasCV/
Email: gabrielas.az@outlook.com
Telephone # 928-567-2120

Hauser Glass Inc

724 Industrial Dr Ste. 8A, Camp Verde,
AZ 86322

Auto Glass Experts

We specialize in all aspect of Auto Glass sourcing
and installation & are dedicated to giving your
fast, friendly and reliable service. Our Technicians
are here to provide expert service and top quality
OEE(original equipment equivalent) or OEM
(original equipment manufacturer). When your
windshield has a chip or crack, bring your car
in to Hauser Glass to have it repaired. We have
competitive pricing, mobile service, licensed
and insured. Services include: Expert Auto Glass
services on all Auto, Truck, Coach, Bus & Custom
Auto Glass. Hauser Glass provides convenient
mobile service to Sedona and the Verde Valley. We
are experts at dealing with insurance companies
and processing claims, easing that particular
headache from the repair process.

Contact Information

Web Address
https://www.hauserglassco.com/
Face Book URL
https://www.facebook.com/Hauser-Glass-105345375245650
Email: hauserglass@yahoo.com
Telephone # 928-567-7549
FAX # 928-567-7687

√ Haven Health of Camp Verde

86 West Salt Mine Road
Our caring professionals provide skilled nursing,
physical therapy, occupational therapy, speech
language pathology, wound care and other
rehabilitation services to help you or your
loved one regain confidence, functionality and
independence. Schedule a tour of the facility.

Contact Information

Web Address
https://www.havenhealthaz.com/locations/camp-
verde/
Face Book URL
https://www.facebook.com/havenhealthgroup
Telephone # 928-567-5253

Hillside Canine Resort and Spa

Hillside K-9 Academy
874 N. Industrial Drive
All of our services are available at this time.
Day-time phone number for take-out, delivery,
appointment, etc.

Contact Information

Web Address
https://www.hillsidecanineresortandspa.com/
Face Book URL
https://www.facebook.com/hillsidecanine
Email: jennifer@hillsidecanine.com
Telephone # 928-567-6304

Independent Vital Life LLC

661 E Howards Rd
Camp Verde, AZ 86322
Vitamins

Contact Information

Web Address
https://www.ivl.com/
Telephone # 928-567-5175

Inge'S Uniquly Warm Caring Home

1625 S Sullivan Lane
Camp Verde, AZ 86322
IngeCare is a licensed Assisted Living home where
residents are invited to live life together with other
seniors and are cared for by loving staff assisting
them with: cleaning, bathing, eating and just plain
enjoying life in a loving home.

Contact Information

Web Address
https://ingecareassistedliving.com/
Email: inge@ingecareassistedliving.com
Telephone # 928-554-1943

Institute for Vibrant Living

661 Howard Rd.
Independent Vital Life LLC (IVL.com) is
the leading direct to consumer vitamin and
supplement company that address specific anti-
aging and health concerns. IVL.com is dedicated
to creating premium quality vitamin supplements
based on the latest health research from America's
leading doctors.

Contact Information

Face Book URL
https://www.facebook.com/IVLLifestyle/
Telephone # 928-567-5175

Camp Verde Business-HWY 260 East of I-17

Integrity Auto Techs Auto and Diesel Repair

873 East Howard Rd. Ste 14
Over 14 Years of Automotive Repair and Emergency Roadside Services in the Verde Valley. Automotive and Diesel master mechanic with ASE Certification. We are also a mobile service we try to save our customers the cost of a tow bill. We offer 24-7 roadside assistance. We operate on an appointment-only basis with the exception of our 24-7 roadside service.
Contact Information
Telephone # 928-444-6294

J&J Machine & Tool

712 Monte Verde Lane
Buy and sell used metal machinery
Contact Information
Telephone # 928-567-0170

John Graves Propane Of Az Inc

Address: 3591 Old Hwy 279
Camp Verde, AZ 86322
We are proud to offer:Propane Delivery Service | Propane Tank Rentals | Propane Accessories & Appliances
Contact Information
Web Address
https://www.johngravespropane.com/
Telephone # 928-567-2425

Jordan'S Hd Towing & Gears

Address:1561 Reeves Arena Rd
Camp Verde, AZ 86322
Towing and Wrecker Service
Contact Information
Telephone # 928-567-6320

Jordan's Heavy Duty Towing

411 E. Howards Rd.
Truck and Tractor-Transmissions
Contact Information
Telephone # 928-567-6320

Little Caesar's

1673 W. State Route 260
Pizza
Hours 10a-10p Take-Out
Contact Information
Web Address
https://littlecaesars.com/en-us/
Face Book URL
https://www.facebook.com/LittleCaesars
Telephone # 928-567-3165

Manife Mini Storage

1566 Sullivan Rd.
Gates open 7 days a week 7A-7P
Contact Information
Telephone # 928-567-9429

McDonald's

1703 W. State Route 260
Open Daily 4A-12A
Take out, drive-through window
Contact Information
Web Address
www.mcdonalds.com
Telephone # 928-567-4388

Mcdonald Bros Construction

Address:1535 S Quarterhorse Ln
Camp Verde, AZ 86322
We specialize in excavation and earth moving technology. Appropriate upfront planning and value engineering are going to keep your project on budget. At McDonald Bros Construction Inc, we are committed to integrity, professional service, and helping you, keep your project on track.
Contact Information
Web Address
http://www.mcdonaldbrosaz.com/
Email: mcdonald@mcdonaldbrosaz.com
Telephone # 928-567-3539
Fax 928-567-6171

Mjb Electric Inc

3680 S Ocotillo Lane
Camp Verde, AZ 86322
Contact Information
Telephone # 602-278-2191

Mjp Contractors LLC

661 E Howards Rd Ste A
Camp Verde, AZ 86322
Contact Information
Telephone # 928-220-0003

√ Montana Mercantile

873 Howards Rd Ste 22, Camp Verde, AZ 86322
Bringing the spirit of the new West to the Verde Valley. Offering apparel, jewelry and gifts!
Contact Information
Face Book URL
https://www.facebook.com/montanamercantileaz/
Email: jchaney.cavecreek@gmail.com
Telephone # 480-720-2565

Mulcaire & Son Contracting LLC

851 Howard Rd.
A freight shipping Trucking Company from CAMP VERDE, AZ. Company USDOT number is 1827659. Transportation Services provided: Flatbed
Contact Information
Web Address
https://partnercarrier.com/AZ/CAMP-VERDE/ MULCAIRE---SON-CONTRACTING-LLC- USDOT-1827659
Telephone # 928-567-2380

NaturMed Inc.

661 Howard Rd. Suite C
Health supplements
Contact Information
Web Address
https://www.ivl.com/
Telephone # 928-567-5175

Nice Jon's Inc

3640 S. Clear water Dr.
Portable toilet supplier and service. Nicest Johns in the west. Satisfaction guaranteed.
7A-6P M-F
Contact Information
Web Address
https://nicejonsaz.com/
Telephone # 928-330-8707

North Horizon Plumbing

725 Howards Road H Camp Verde, AZ 86322;

- Residential & Commercial Plumbing

- License Bonded and Insured

- New Construction, Remodels, Service Plumbing

Open 24 hr

Contact Information

Web Address

https://north-horizon-plumbing.business.site/

Face Book URL

https://www.facebook.com/North-Horizon-Plumbing-267171600075426/

Email: northhorizonplumbing@yahoo.com

Telephone # 928-567-6675

———————————

Northern Arizona Mold Inspector

2210 Westward Dr

Camp Verde, AZ 86322

Mailing Address:

522 W. Finnie Flat Rd. Suite E. #148

Camp Verde, AZ 86322

Home Inspection-Take the first step in a healthier home, by having your home inspection by a Mold Assessment Consultant.

Testing-I use the most advanced labs to accurately test your home for mold.

Plan of Action-If mold is found in your home, I will create an effective plan of action to have it removed.

Follow Up-I make sure the job is done right with a follow up inspection after the removal process.

Contact Information

Web Address

http://northernarizonamoldinspector.com/

Telephone # 928- 224-2988

Northern Hardscape LLC

873 Howards Rd Ste #5, Camp Verde, AZ 86322

Northern Hardscape is known for its quality landscaping because we approach every project with care and meticulous detail. We believe in building lasting relationships with our clients, that can bring their dream yards come true.

Landscape Installation; There's a reason why we're a top Landscaping Service. From clean-up projects to full yard remodels, we approach every project with expertise and care. You can count on us to make sure you're satisfied with the results. Just ask our valued customers! Contact us to learn more.

Yard Clean-Up; We specialize in Yard Clean-Up services to get your yard back to its former glory. Debris haul away service is available.

Irrigation Installation Our Irrigation services provide solutions for a variety of outdoor spaces. We cater to the needs and requirements of each and every client, guaranteeing you'll get exactly what you want.

Patio & Paver Installation Have a yard that needs to be transformed into an outdoor living space? We have your solution with Patios and Paver Design and Installation services.

Contact Information

Web Address

https://www.northernhardscapeaz.com/

Face Book URL

https://www.facebook.com/Northernhardscapellc

Email: northernhardscapellc@gmail.com

Telephone # 928-968-3111

———————————

Camp Verde Business-HWY 260 East of I-17

On The Go Auto Repair

4561 E Canyon Drive
Camp Verde, AZ 86322
Contact Information
Telephone # 928-649-9065

Oothoudt Brothers Inc

823 N Industrial Dr
Camp Verde, AZ 86322
Trucking company located in Camp Verde, AZ.
Road construction and Dirt hauling.

Contact Information
Face Book URL
https://www.facebook.com/Oothoudtbros/
Telephone # 928-567-2656

Painless Stitches Upholstery

873 East Howard Rd. Ste 1
Patio and indoor furniture, airplanes, automotive,
motorcycles, boats and watercraft and everything
in between. 9A-5P M-F
Contact Information
Web Address
http://painlessstitchesupholstery.com/
Face Book URL
https://www.facebook.com/
painlessstitchesupholstery/
Email: painlessstitchesupholstery@gmail.com
Telephone # 928-567-2308

Parker Construction Enterprise

1567 Murdock Rd
Camp Verde, AZ 86322
Services Provided by Parker Construction
Enterprises: Septic Tank Pumping, Sewer Systems,
Porta Potty Rental, Waste Disposal, Grease
Trap Cleaning, Cesspool Pumping, Septic Tank
Installation, Septic System Construction
Contact Information
Web Address
https://www.septic.com/septic-services/arizona/
camp-verde/parker-construction-enterprises/
Telephone # 928-567-3769

Peejay Plumbing Heating & Fire

454 E Old Cowboy Ln, Camp Verde, AZ 86322
Cross Streets: Near the intersection of E Old
Cowboy Ln and S Reeves Arena Rd
Plumbing, Plumbing Contractor
Heating & Fire Protection, Inc. is a company
incorporated in Arizona and its File ID is
09891599.
Contact Information
Email: Not Available
Telephone # 928-567-1999

Petrie Contracting LLC

Address:1454 Vail Rd
Camp Verde, AZ 86322General Contractor,
Custom Homes, Remodel, Carpentry.
Contact Information
Face Book URL
https://www.facebook.com/
PetriecontractingLLC/
Email: tyson@petriecontracting.com
Telephone # 928-301-3226

PIEH Tool Company Inc.

661 E. Howard Rd. Ste J
 Artists, blacksmith supplies, farrier, equine, bovine & Veterinary supplies. *Artistic Blacksmithing classes. Take home 6-12 finished projects in 3 days. 8A-5P M-F, Sat by appointment.

Contact Information

Web Address
https://piehtoolco.com/
Face Book URL
https://www.facebook.com/piehtoolco/
Email: piehtoolinfo@piehtoolco.com
Telephone # 928-554-0700
Phone Orders 888-743-4866,
FAX Orders 928-554-0800

Pierce Builders LLC

216 E Quarterhorse
Camp Verde, AZ 86322
General Contractor, Custom Homes, Remodel, Carpentry

Contact Information

Telephone # 928-301-3226

Plowing Ahead Ranch

4120 West Mahoney Rd
Camp Verde
Here at Plowing Ahead Ranch, we believe in living simply but living fully. What does this mean? To us it means living our lives enjoying the simple pleasures afforded us by living in harmony with the land, with our livestock and with native wildlife.

Contact Information

Web Address
https://plowingaheadranch.com/
Face Book URL
https://www.facebook.com/PlowingAheadRanch/
Email: plowingahead.az@gmail.com
Telephone # 928-300-3062

Quintus Inc

684 Industrial Dr
Camp Verde, AZ 86322
Quintus is a contract manufacturer with a proven history in the design, prototype and production of composite products for a variety of applications and industries. We also offer carbon fiber rods and plates as standard catalog items. Prototyping, machining, pad printing, laser etching, component assembly.

Contact Information

Web Address
http://www.quintus-inc.com/
Telephone # 928-567-3833

R & K Custom Homes
Address:496 E Quarterhorse
Camp Verde, AZ 86322
Contact Information
Telephone # 928-821-1704

____

Rayburn Electric LLC
Camp Verde, AZ
Rayburn Electric in Camp Verde is here to
serve you. We are a Licensed Contractor (ROC
331937), so you know we will provide quality
workmanship, and a quality experience. For
all of your electrical needs both in the house
and outdoors call us today. Residential and
Commercial Calls are welcome!
Contact Information
Email: Not Available
Telephone # 928-713-3614

____

Remick Law PLC
661 E Howards Rd B3, Camp Verde

Lawyer, Business Law. Call for an appointment.
Contact Information
Telephone # 928-239-1780

____

Rise N' Shine House Cleaning
Camp Verde
Areas served: Camp Verde and nearby areas. My
mission is to leave your house spotless so that
all you have to do is Rise and Shine. If you are
interested in a one-time, as needed, or weekly
cleaning for your home, office or vacation rental,
call or text us!
Contact Information
Email: Not Available
Telephone # 928-592-2064

____

Road Runner Rentals
891 Howard Rd.
Yard Equipment Rentals
Contact Information
Telephone # 928-567-3739

____

Robinson Golf Cars
725 E Howards Rd.
Robinson Golf Cars have been a family-owned
and operated business since 1989. We carry the
largest inventory of both new and used, electric
and gas, vehicles in Northern Arizona with many
golf cart makes and models in stock. 8A-4P M-F
Contact Information
Web Address
https://arizonagolfcars.com/
Face Book URL
https://www.facebook.com/robinsongolfcars
Email: info@arizonagolfcars.com
Telephone # 928-567-3100

____

Rocky Construction Excavation
1095 East Rancho Rd.
Rocky Construction, based out of Camp Verde,
AZ, is an excavation contractor that provides
septic/leach drain field installation, storm shelter
design and demolition services. Our professionals
work tirelessly to leave lasting, quality results.
If you're in the market for top-tier residential
services, let our friendly staff know about your
project. Demolition Services: Barn Demolition,
Mobile Home Demolition, Excavation, Septic
Systems.
Contact Information
Web Address
https://www.hometowndemolitioncontractors.com/
demolition-reviews/rocky-construction-inc-camp-
verde-az.html
Telephone # 928-567-6597

____

Camp Verde Business-HWY 260 East of I-17

Roto-Fab LLC

921 E. Howards Rd
Camp Verde, AZ 86322
Accessory covers, air intake systems, air scoops, apparel, big gulp series, ls engine swaps, oil caps, replacement parts. Roto-fab is excited to offer our newest addition to the Big Gulp® Series of cold air intake systems! With duct work nearly 20% larger in diameter than our standard 2012-15 ZL1 CAI, the Big Gulp® CAI was designed to meet the air demands of the fastest Camaros in the world. Don't leave horsepower on the table - get the most out of your modifications.

Contact Information
Web Address
https://www.roto-fab.com/
Face Book URL
https://www.facebook.com/rotofab/
Email: sales@roto-fab.com
Telephone # 260-375-4480

____

Route 66 Images

Address: 4215 E Clear Creek Dr
Camp Verde, AZ 86322
Contact Information
Face Book URL
https://www.facebook.com/route66images
Email: route66images@gmail.com
Telephone # 602-570-8157

____

Ruby Road Resale Mall

851 E Howard Rd.
Antiques and collectibles. One-of-a-kind treasures in over 6000 square feet. 10A-6P (Usual Hours)
Contact Information
Web Address
https://www.rubyroadresale.com/
Face Book URL
https://www.facebook.com/RubyRoadResale
Email: shoprubyroad@gmail.com
Telephone # 928-567-5759

Salt Mine Wine

Physical address: 536 W. Salt Mine Road
Camp Verde AZ 86322
Mailing address: PO Box 2840, Camp Verde, AZ 86322
We are a small family-owned vineyard and winery in Camp Verde, Arizona. In 2013, the Norton family selected an historic farm site as a future vineyard and winery. Over the next three years, we planted five acres of grapes compatible with our growing season, soils and micro climate. Today, nestled in among pecan groves, pastures, small farms and roadside produce stands we specialize in growing Italian varietals such as Malvasia Bianca and Sangiovese. Please call our Tasting Room at 928-910-2075 or e-mail info@saltminewine.com.

Contact Information
Web Address
https://www.saltminewine.com/
Face Book URL
https://www.facebook.com/saltminewine
Email: kevin.norton@saltminewine.com
Email: info@saltminewine.com
Telephone # 928-910-2075

____

Seekins Enterprises

715 Stolen Blvd
Camp Verde, AZ 86322
Arizona Transport Company. Cargo Hauling: Motor Vehicles, Lumber, Building Materials, Machinery
Contact Information
Telephone # 928-567-9102
FAX 928-567-0413

Sinagua Malt

573 Industrial Drive
Camp Verde, AZ 86322
Sinagua Malt is a benefit corporation located in Camp Verde, Arizona. Sinagua Malt was created to provide a market solution for declining flows in the Verde River. We provide breweries, distilleries, and homebrew-supply stores with premium Arizona malt.

Contact Information

Web Address
https://www.sinaguamalt.com/
Face Book URL
https://www.facebook.com/sinaguamalt
Email: info@sinaguamalt.com
Email: sales@sinaguamalt.com
Telephone # 928-300-9013 480-878-9583

Specialty Powder Coating

Address:4900 N Hayfield Draw #A
Camp Verde, AZ 86322
We offer Sandblasting and Powder Coating services, for anything from a 25' Structural beam for Mr. Contractor guy, all the way down to the Misses lawn furniture.
Phone: # 928-567-2130
Contact Information
Face Book URL
https://www.facebook.com/Specialty-Powder-Coating-Sandblasting-106978657438447/
Email: dan16spc@gmail.com
Telephone # 928-567-2130

Stallings Performance Horses

Address: Jackpot Ranch
2025 W Reservation Loop Rd, Camp Verde, AZ 86322 Camp Verde, AZ 86322
Equine Rehab- Our personalized rehab programs include just the right combination of services to meet you and your horse's specific needs. We can offer BEMER therapy, a hot walker, on-site care, expert veterinary service, transition from rehab to training, and flexible living including accommodations for stall rest.
Pasture and Stall Boarding-We offer a variety of choices for boarding your horse. Whether you're looking for a long-term home, or seeking to get out of the snow in the winter or the heat in the summer, your horse will simply love our place. Our facility offers barn stalls, mare motel stalls, and full-time pasture board. Each horse boarded in our stalls are rotated through our green pastures each day. **Clinics-**We offer a variety of clinics with focus on anything from general horsemanship, cow work, cutting, reining, barrels, roping, sorting, penning, and shooting. Contact us for more details.
Private and Group Lessons-We offer private lessons at our facility, riding with Kevin and his team.
Horse Showing-We'll show your horse to meet whatever show goals you might have. Kevin Stallings trains colts from start to finish; from the first ride to a finished working cow horse, reiner, barrel horse, cutter or other performance horse.
Horse Training-Whether starting a colt, tuning up before an event or creating your winning show horse, we'll design a training program to meet your needs.
Contact Information
Web Address
http://www.stallingsperformancehorses.com/
Face Book URL
https://www.facebook.com/StallingsPerformanceHorses/?ref=page_internal
Email: kevin@dakotacom.net
Telephone # 520-906-4852

Camp Verde Business-HWY 260 East of I-17

√ Starbucks I-17

1620 State Route 260
Coffee, pastries
4A-8:30P Every Day
Drive Through, Dine-in, Dine on porch
Contact Information
Web Address
https://www.starbucks.com/
Telephone # 928-567-0274

Subway

In Shell Station
1673 W. Hwy 260
Sandwiches. Hours 730a-930pm, Take-out
Contact Information
Web Address
https://restaurants.subway.com/
Telephone # 928-567-2315

Sweet Pea Antiques

437 W. Hwy 260
Sweet Pea is welcome to all things, old, kitchy, vintage and antique! We have 10,000 square feet of retail space filled with treasures, up-cycled, reused, and refurbished. With over 40 vendors we offer thousands of items big or small. New displays every week. 7 days a week. 10A-5P
Contact Information
Web Address
https://sweetpeatrading.com/
Face Book URL
https://www.facebook.com/SweetPeaTradingLLC
Email: sweetpeatradingllc@gmail.com
Telephone # 928-567-6555

Swift Roofing

873 East Howard Rd. Ste 7
Performance + Quality + Expertise = Roofing Perfection. We Can Help You With All Your Roofing Needs. Our team has over 15+ years of combined experience building & repairing custom roofs. AZ ROC 324945 - Licensed & Bonded. CALL US TODAY FOR AN ESTIMATE: 928 592-3693   Hrs. 7A-5P M-F, 7A-3P Sat
Contact Information
Web Address
https://swiftroofingllc.com/
Face Book URL
https://www.facebook.com/swiftroofing1989
Email: swiftroofing1989@gmail.com
Telephone # 928-308-1955

Taco Bell

1602 W Hwy 260
Mexican Fast Food
Hours 7A-10P daily
Take out, drive-through window, dine-in
Contact Information
Web Address
locations.tacobell.com
Telephone # 928-554-0233

Tamara's Nails to Tails Salon

Professional Canine Grooming
873 East Howard Rd. Ste 18
Contact Information
Face Book URL
https://www.facebook.com/Tamaras-Nails-To-Tails-Salon-1831076773821249/
Telephone # 928-592-3832

Temp Storage LLC

1494 Davidson
Camp Verde, AZ 86322
Whether it's for a long or short period of time, we are here to make your storage experience as easy as possible by offering a full range of products and services to meet your storage needs at an affordable price. Simply reserve a unit online or come by and see us today! Mon-Fri: 12:00 AM - 11:59 PM, Sat: 12:00 AM - 11:59 PM, Sun: 12:00 AM - 11:59 PM
Contact Information
Web Address
https://www.sitelinkstore.com/Temp-Storage/933
Email: tempstorage@yahoo.com
Telephone # 928-351-6699

The Fish's Garden

393 W. Grippen Road
Mail: P.O. Box 4170
Local fish and produce growers using a science-based aquaponics system.
Contact Information
Web Address
https://www.thefishsgarden.com
Face Book URL
https://www.facebook.com/TFGaquaponics/
Telephone # 928-301-4337

The Jr's Auto Detail

873 Howards Rd.
Camp Verde
Telephone # 928-254-7949

Triple X Construction Inc

Camp Verde, AZ 86322
AZ Home Builder and Experts in Custom Home Construction in Camp Verde, Sedona, Cottonwood, and Prescott, Arizona
Delivering stunning residences is our way of life at Triple X Construction. Our company is a full service general contractor with over a decade of experience in custom home construction in Camp Verde, Sedona, Cottonwood, and Prescott, Arizona. Certifications:
> General Commercial Contractor Class B-01 License
> General Residential Contractor Class B-02 License
> A General Engineering License
> MSHA Certified
> CR10 Drywall and Light Gauge Framing
> A – Engineering license in progress

Contact Information
Web Address
https://triplexconstructionaz.com/
Face Book URL
https://www.facebook.com/Triple-x-Construction-Inc-109183268183226
Email: triplexconst@msn.com
Telephone # 928-567-5180

Camp Verde Business-HWY 260 East of I-17

Two Feet Beyond Inc

Address: 285 Pheasant Run Cir
Camp Verde, AZ 86322
Two Feet Beyond provides customized personal apparel, promotional products. Products are sublimated, screen printed and pad printed.

Contact Information

Web Address
https://www.twofeetbeyond.com/
Email: twofeetbeyond@aol.com
Telephone # 928-592-9137
FAX: 928-567-4025

Ultimate Cart and Dolly

724 Industrial Dr Suite 7B, Camp Verde, AZ
Ultimate Cart and Dolly has designed an industrial cart and industrial dolly that can protect your workers from injury and improve employee productivity. Move over 1200 lbs. over any terrain with ease.

Contact Information

Web Address
https://ultimatecartanddolly.com/
Face Book URL
https://www.facebook.com/Ultimatecartanddolly
Email: courtney@ultimatecartanddolly.com
Telephone # 928-300-5879

√ Verde Brewing Co.

724 N. Industrial Drive Unit 7A
Appetizers, burgers, and craft beer
Inside dining, outside dining, Take-out. 11A-9P

Contact Information

Web Address
https://www.verdebrewing.com/
Telephone # 928-567-8626

Valley Performance

2943 Palo Verde Ln, Camp Verde, AZ 86322
Quality Service! Fair Rates! We'll Come to You! Valley Performance - providing top quality shop and mobile auto repair to Camp Verde, the Verde Valley and Northern Arizona. If you need dependable, dedicated, honest, local mechanic service, you've come to the right place. Whether it's a minor or major, on-site, roadside, or in-shop repair, we'll get you back on the road as quickly and painlessly as possible.

Contact Information

Web Address
http://valleyperformance.net/index.html
Email: Not Available
Telephone # 928-254-8042

√ Verde Ranch Estates

10 S. Monarch Ln Camp Verde AZ 86322

See yourself here! Our newly constructed, all-ages neighborhood is taking shape in Camp Verde, Arizona – "the heart of it all." Just 90 minutes from Phoenix and a short ride to Cottonwood, Sedona, and Flagstaff. Beautifully appointed, 3-bedroom, 2-bath homes with front porches are just the beginning of the story. The magic of living at Verde Ranch Estates comes into focus through the luxury of on-site amenities such as:

- Clubhouse
- Pool and Hot tub
- Fitness center
- Pet park
- Pickleball courts
- Playground
- Walking and biking trails

Contact Information
Web Address
https://verderanchestates.com/
Email: vreinfo@crrmgmt.com
Telephone # 928-291-2418

____

√ Verde Ranch RV Storage

162 N Goswick Way, Camp Verde, AZ 86322
Paved Lot, Covered Spaces, Security system located conveniently between Sedona, Flagstaff and Phoenix. We offer Sewage Dump Station, Vehicle Wash Bays, Electrical Charging Station, Water Filling Station, Air Compressor Commercial Grade for Regular and High Pressure Tires. Hours: Monday-Friday 9AM–5PM, Saturday 9AM–4PM, Sunday Closed
Contact Information
Web Address
https://verderanchrvstorage.com/
Telephone # 928-792-4458

____

Verde Sol Air Services

724 Industrial Drive
Air Conditioning Contractor, Heating and AC, Plumbing, Solar, Duct Cleaning. M-F 7A-4P
Contact Information
Web Address
https://verdesolair.com/
Telephone # 928-567-5315

____

Wendy's

1897 Pueblo Ridge Suite C
Burgers, fast food
Take-out, Dine-in, Drive Through window
Contact Information
Web Address
https://www.wendys.com/home
Face Book URL
https://www.facebook.com/wendys/
Telephone # 928-567-9276

____

Yavapai Apache Whitehills

320 Castle Ln
Camp Verde, AZ 86322
Contact Information
Web Address
https://yavapai-apache.org/
Telephone # 928-554-0731

____

Your Neighborhood Handyman

312 W Hereford Drive
Camp Verde, AZ 86322
Contact Information
Telephone # 775-54-6805

____

Reserved add space for Chamber adds.

Call to reserve space. Must be a member.

1/4 Page $100, 1/2 Page $200, Full Page $400

Reserved add space for Chamber adds.

Call to reserve space. Must be a member.

1/4 Page $100, 1/2 Page $200, Full Page $400

Camp Verde Business-HWY 260 West of I-17

Zane Grey RV Village

4500 E, AZ-260, Camp Verde, AZ 86322
A Beautiful Northern Arizona RV Park and Cabin Rental resort near Sedona and the Red Rock attractions. Comfortable RV camping sites on West Clear Creek in Camp Verde, Arizona. The location is unique, with a creek-side path and lots of shade. Our friendly staff will make your stay comfortable and enjoyable. Zane Grey RV Village is open year round to meet your Arizona vacation needs in any season.

Contact Information

Web Address

https://www.zanegreyrv.com/?utm_source=google.com&utm_medium=organic&utm_campaign=GMB_Listing_Clicks

Face Book URL

https://www.facebook.com/ZaneGreyRVVillage/

Telephone # 928-567-4320

____

Zane Grey Storage

660 East Howard Rd.
Storage Facility in Camp Verde
Mon-Thur 8A-3P, Fri 8A-12P, Sat and Sun by apt.
Gate 6A-7:30P Daily

Contact Information

Web Address

http://www.storagefront.com/self-storage/arizona/camp-verde/zane-grey-mini-storage-and-commercial-complex-112357

Face Book URL

https://www.facebook.com/ZGministorage/

Telephone # 928-567-8566

→Hwy 260 West of I-17

2 Brothers Boat & Rv Storage

1555 Parish Lane, Camp Verde, Az 86322
Company specialized in: Recreational Vehicle Storage.

Contact Information

Email: Not Available

Telephone # 928-567-6331

____

A-1 Affordable Mini & RV Storage

3702 W Hwy 260
Office Hours Sun 10:00 AM - 2:00 PM Mon-Sat 9A-5P

Contact Information

Web Address

https://www.armored-mini-storage.com/self-storage-camp-verde-az-129044

Face Book URL

https://www.facebook.com/campverdestorage/

Email: a.1storage@yahoo.com

Telephone # 928-224-1549

____

AGM Power Systems

4565 W. Old Corral Lane
Primary power systems, custom-built standby power units, generators, RV generators, portable generators, switching units, portable rental generators. Mon-Thu: 8am – 4pm, Fri: 8am – 2pm, Sat-Sun: Closed.

Contact Information

Web Address

https://agmpowersystem.com/

Email: info@agmpowersupply.com

Telephone # 928-634-2223

Arizona Exposure Marketing

2445 N Belgian Way, Camp Verde, AZ
As a full service agency we can help with marketing and advertising planning, branding your businesses and so much more!   Even if you hire us for just one of our services, we always consider how that piece fits within your larger communications strategy. It is that type of integrated thinking that's allowed a small agency like us to be in this business for over 25 years and help our clients achieve their objectives.

Contact Information

Web Address
https://arizonaexposure.com/
Face Book URL
https://www.facebook.com/ArizonaThingsToDo/
Email: map@arizonaexposure.com
Telephone # 928-607-12133

Arizona Jobsite Concrete LLC

3900 W Cherry Creek Rd, Camp Verde AZ 86322
Since the late 1990's, AJC has been offering concrete delivery services to the Verde Valley and surrounding areas. The owner, Randy Torman began operations with a single volumetric mixer and specialized in small projects where orders averaged between one and four yards of concrete. As the area grew and the demand for concrete increased, AJC purchased two additional volumetic mixers to service the small order market.

Contact Information

Web Address
http://www.arizonajobsiteconcrete.com/About-Us.html
Face Book URL https://www.facebook.com/azjobsiteconcrete/
Telephone # 928-649-0602

Arizona Recovery and Towing

3611 Old Highway 279, Camp Verde AZ 86322
We are a professional Towing company serving all of Camp Verde, Cottonwood, Sedona, Mayer, Oak Creek, Munds Park, Rimrock, Jerome, Clarkdale, Dewey, Humboldt, Cornville, and the surrounding areas.

*   Great Rates!!!

*   Speedy And Polite, Professional Service

*   We Specialize In Luxury And High End Vehicles

*   24 Hour Fast Response Towing And Roadside Service

*   RV, Boat Towing And Equipment Hauling Available

Towing
We specialize in Auto Towing, Truck Towing, Flatbed Towing, Light & Medium Duty Towing, RV, Boat and Motorcycle Towing. We provide Local and Out-of-town Tows and hauling. Give us a call for a quote and for all your Towing needs! Call us first for a fast quote or pick up!

Contact Information

Face Book URL
https://www.facebook.com/azrecoveryandtowing
Email: azrecoveryandtowing@yahoo.com
Telephone # 928-300-9899

Camp Verde Business-HWY 260 West of I-17

Arizona State Concrete LLC

2872 S. Aspen Way, Camp Verde Az 86322
Proudly licensed, bonded, and insured. ROC
292544. Serving the Verde Valley and Northern
AZ since 2005 with over 20 years in the trade,
we are experts in new concrete construction and
repairs (footings, stem walls, interior and exterior
work, driveways, patios, sidewalks, pool decks,
stamped concrete, etc.) Also available for skid
steer work, haul off, grading, and resolution of
drainage issue.
Contact Information
Web Address
https://www.sedonalimodriver.com/
Face Book URL
https://www.facebook.com/arizonastateconcrete/
Email: Jayssonchurch@gmail.com
Telephone # 928-821-0953

Arizona Zip Lines LLC

4020 N Cherry Road, Camp Verde, AZ
Located: 3505 West State Route 260, @ Out of
Africa, Camp Verde, AZ
Experience the wind whipping through your hair
on a thrill ride over nature's wildest predators.
Enjoy the adventure of a lifetime on a world-class
zip line over Out of Africa Wildlife Park in Camp
Verde, Arizona! We are conveniently located
less than 20 miles from Sedona, in the heart of
Northern Arizona's wine country, just minutes
from tasting rooms and vineyards. From the top
of the towers, you can see majestic red rocks, the
San Francisco peaks, and the whole breathtaking
Verde Valley including Cottonwood, Clarkdale,
and Jerome. Ride the most exciting zip line ever
devised, over Out of Africa, and soar over lions,
tigers, wolves, hyenas, bears, leopards, cougars
and other natural predators! Book the most
exciting Arizona zip lining experience yet!
Contact Information
Web Address
https://predatorzipline.com/

Face Book URL
https://www.facebook.com/ZipOutofAfrica
Email: info@predatorzipline.com
Telephone # 928-567-9947

Audio Visual Specialists LLC

2435 N. Arturo Cir. E, Camp Verde, Az 86322
Professional AV Solutions For ALL Building
Types and Budgets! Audio Visual Specialists is
dedicated to providing our customers with high
quality, reliable, cost effective and "user friendly"
solutions for their audio-visual system needs. We
recognize that providing unparalleled customer
and technical service is the key to achieving and
maintaining a leadership position in the Audio-
Visual Industry. We are committed to developing
long-standing relationships with our customers
and providing continued support and service
with professional courtesy and hometown trust.
With over 30 years working Live / Concert and
Corporate AV events and over 14 years providing
Audio Visual System Design-Engineering,
Integration and Installation services, our years of
experience means that we know what works. Give
us a call today to discuss how we can make your
project / event a success!
Contact Information
Web Address
https://www.avscorp.net/
Face Book URL
https://www.facebook.com/
audiovideosolutionscorporation/
Telephone # 928-649-0166

Camp Verde Business-HWY 260 West of I-17

Bella Notte Concierge LLC

4001 Old Hwy 279. Camp Verde, AZ 86322
Total corporate transparency is a critical requirement for a fairer society. To ensure that everyone knows exactly who they are working with and working for. To tackle corruption and criminality. To protect our democracy.

Contact Information

Web Address
https://opencorporates.com/companies/us_az/23185273
Email: Not Available
Telephone # Not Available

____

Cherry Creek RV Storage LLC

Address: 3900 N Cherry Creek Rd
Camp Verde, AZ 86322
RV Storage conveniently located 3.5 miles from Interstate 17

- On-Site Manager
- Keypad Gated Entry
- 24 Hour Access
- Low Monthly Rate
- Locally Owned

Contact Information

Face Book URL
https://www.facebook.com/pages/category/Self-Storage-Facility/Cherry-Creek-RV-Storage-105297867590263/
Telephone # 928-567-3046

____

Cloverleaf RV Village

33380 W. Cloverleaf Ranch Road
Long term spaces for those looking for a small quiet place to park by the Verde River. We encourage alternative and vintage housing options. Adults only, over 18. Tiny homes are welcome. Wifi, Water, septic, trash, electric.

Contact Information

Web Address
https://cloverleafrvvillage.com/
Email: 3380cloverleaf@gmail.com
Telephone # 928-853-3553

____

Conoco Gas Station and Market Place

3400 Hwy 260
Gas Station and Convenience Store

Contact Information

Web Address
https://www.conoco.com/
Telephone # 928-567-8881

____

Copper Star Indoor Shooting Range

3535 W. Sharp Shooter Way.
25 Yard, 50 Yard, 100 Yard Indoor shooting range. Rental, Firearms, and Bows. Gun Safety Classes Thur-Mon 10A-6P

Contact Information

Web Address
http://copperstarisr.com/
Face Book URL
https://www.facebook.com/Copper-Star-Indoor-Shooting-Range-242592732430599/
Email: copperstarleader@gmail.com
Telephone # 928-567-5300

____

Camp Verde Business-HWY 260 West of I-17

Cree Windmills

2857 Aspen Way, Camp Verde, AZ 86322
American made in Camp Verde, Arizona, now
in Escondido, California. Wooden Windmills,
Bird Feeders and Bird Houses. Made of recycled,
distressed and new wood. Hand-made and hand-
painted gifts to add to the beauty and enjoyment of
any Outdoor Living space.
All 8ft windmills are made of distressed, recycled
and new wood. The "Base" is waterproofed with
several coats of stain of "Behr Waterproofing
for Decks" and the Petals/Blades are Primed and
painted with Rust-oleum paint . They are made
to order, one at a time, taking 3/4 weeks to build.
You can order one offered in the shop or pick any
style that is available, or you may want to request
a certain style in the color combination of your
choice, like a green color base with any of the
heads, like the "Sunflower" (petals/blades styles).
Color preferences can be done at no extra cost,
with a style you may want. You can order through
Messenger, Comments, email cree.windmills@
outlook.com, call or text 602.810.0344.

Contact Information

Face Book URL
https://www.facebook.com/creewindmills
Instagram: https://www.instagram.com/cree.
lOh4tPzxPguDs6eNOfl9eYwBM6hgeejTYj38GI
Email: cree.windmills@outlook.com
Telephone # 602-810-0344

____

Epone Equine LLC

1666 S Sullivan Ln, Camp Verde AZ
Epona Equine LLC was founded in 2012.
Additional information is available at or by
contacting Laurie M Brander at 928-554-4244.

Contact Information

Telephone # 928-554-4244

____

Fasteen Farms

2093 Paso Fino Way
Camp Verde, AZ 86322
Purveyor of locally grown produce and makers of
home canned products.

Contact Information

Face Book URL
https://www.facebook.com/fasteenfarms
Email: fasteen@msn.com
Telephone # 612-272-0084

____

FD Creative Designs

1487 W Horseshoe Bend
Camp Verde, AZ 86322
Accessories and wear.

Contact Information

Web Address
https://www.etsy.com/shop/fdcreativedesigns?fb
clid=IwAR3H7y0o1bKhNBJWFCJBOyT_8Rh--
tJde-iaHVFAk_Gj9U-q2VwGMBcIH2M
Face Book URL
https://www.facebook.com/fdcreativedesigns/
Email: fdcreativedesings@gmail.com

____

French's RV Center

Address:3702 W Hwy 260 #B
Camp Verde, AZ 86322
Our friendly, experienced service department will
keep your RV in top condition.

Contact Information

Web Address
http://www.frenchsrv.com/
Email: frenchsrv@icloud.com
Telephone # 928-567-0055

____

Gardner's Recycling

4740 Old Hwy 279
Camp Verde, AZ 86322
Oldest metal recyclers in the Verde Valley
We accept all types of metal for recycling.
We PAY CASH
Contact Information
Face Book URL
https://www.facebook.com/
GardnersRecycling/
Email: gardnersrecycling@yahoo.com
Telephone # 928-634-5176

Go West Design Co

Address:2357 W Newton Lane
Camp Verde, AZ 86322
Go West Design Co. Specializes in custom logos,
websites and marketing materials that convey your
unique style & message.
Contact Information
Web Address
https://www.gowestdesignco.com/
Telephone # 928-233-6033

Goettls High Desert Mechanical-HVAC & Plumbing Specialists

4650 Old Hwy 279, Camp Verde, AZ 86322
A decades-old leader in the HVAC (heating,
ventilation, and air conditioning) industry, Goettl's
High Desert Mechanical provides premium service
and installation of heating and cooling systems
throughout northern and central Arizona. Our
unwavering commitment to customer satisfaction
began in 1987. Heating and cooling, maintenance,
plumbing. Areas served: Camp Verde and nearby
areas.
Hours: Open 24 hours
Contact Information
Web Address
https://goettlshdm.com/
Face Book URL
https://www.facebook.com/goettlsHDM
Email: office@goettls.com
Telephone # 928-567-2200

Hammes Surveying LLC

Address:2100 Via Silverado
Camp Verde, AZ 86322
Land Surveyor
Contact Information
Telephone # 928-567-2833

Hand Helping Handyman

2075 Park Verde Rd CV
Camp Verde, AZ 86322
Contact Information
Telephone # 928-301-3053

Camp Verde Business-HWY 260 West of I-17

Hansen Ent Fleet Repair LLC

4682 Old Hwy 279
Camp Verde, AZ 86322
We are the Verde Valley's Vehicle Maintenance
Shop.
We are located in Camp Verde, Arizona and
service vehicles from all over Northern Arizona,
including Camp Verde, Cottonwood, Flagstaff,
Phoenix, Prescott, and Sedona. We specialize
in automotive diesel powered vehicles, such
as Ford Power Strokes, Dodge Cummins, and
the Chevrolet Duramax. We are also highly
qualified to work on gasoline powered cars and
pickups.We have the facility and experience to
maintain: cars and pickups, medium duty trucks,
heavy duty trucks and trailers. We have the
diagnostic equipment needed to work on today's
modern computerized vehicles.
Contact Information
Web Address
https://www.hefrshop.com/
Face Book URL
https://www.facebook.com/Hansen-Enterprises-
Fleet-Repair-LLC-103165369750137
Telephone # 928-567-9140

Hugh-Mac Transport Inc

Address:3557 Old Hwy 279
Camp Verde, AZ 86322
Specialized Freight Trucking Industry
Contact Information
Telephone # 928-567-6999

Jones Ford Verde Valley

5980 E. Coury Dr.
Ford sales and service. Jones Arizona's Best Since
1970. For over 50 years, Jones Auto Group has
been known as 'Arizona's Best' car dealership
Arizona. We offer the full Ford line-up, pre-owned
vehicles with the Jones Lifetime Power Train
Protection, and a full Service Department for all
makes and models. Come visit us at 5980 E Coury
Drive, a convenient, centralized location on the
Camp Verde-Bridgeport Highway, HWY 260 only
seven miles NW of the I-17. We hope to see you
soon. M-Sat 8A-6P.
Contact Information
Web Address
https://www.jonesfordverdevalley.com/
Face Book URL
https://www.facebook.com/jonesfordvv
Email: parker@jonesfordverde.com
Telephone #
Sales: 888-476-1766
Service: 833-770-9974
Parts: 888-481-1611

Kaisen Collision Center

1900 N. Moonrise Dr.
Car, truck, and RV collision repair. Life bends
them. We mend them. M-F 8A-5P
Contact Information
Face Book URL
https://www.facebook.com/vincesauto1
E-Mail
email: vincesauto1@aol.com
Telephone # 928-282-1635

KP Ventures Well Drilling & Pump Co

4715 Old Hwy 279, Camp Verde, AZ 86322
KP Ventures is a well drilling and pump service company with 3 locations to serve you (Camp Verde(AZ), Phoenix(AZ), & Wenden (AZ)) We also serve the greater Southwestern US. Our staff are certified well drillers by the National Groundwater Association (NGWA) and we hold 14 well drilling/ pump installer licenses in 8 states. You will not find a more experienced pump service or well drilling contractor in Arizona.

Well Drilling

- Residential Well Drilling
- Commercial and Industrial Well Drilling
- Agricultural/ Irrigation Well Installation
- Mineral Exploration (RC & Diamond Core)
- Monitoring Wells
- Municipal Water Wells

Pump Services

- Residential pump services for 'out of water' or loss of water pressure events. (24/7 Emergency Service Available)

- Vertical Turbine pump repair and service

- Well Rehabilitation & Development

- Booster Pump Replacements and Repair

- Aquifer and Pump Testing

- Well Inspections

- Well Video Services

- Pump system design and manufacture for vertical turbine & submersible applications.

- Cable Tool Well Development

Hours: 8AM-5PM

Contact Information

Web Address
https://www.kpventureswelldrilling.com/
Face Book URL
https://www.facebook.com/KP-Ventures-Well-
Drilling-Pump-Co-1600532893548631/
Email: Not Available
Telephone # 928-639-1709

La Fonda Mexican Food

2750 West Horseshoe Bend Dr.
Mexican Food. Take-out, Dine-in
Tue-Sat 11A-8P, Hours 10a-10p Take-Out

Contact Information

Face Book URL
https://www.facebook.com/La-Casita-240420636160416/
Telephone # 928-567-3500

Ligon Excavation Inc

39900 Hayfield Draw Rd. Camp Verde, AZ 86322
Combining years of experience with a dedication to client satisfaction, Ligon Excavation Inc has established itself as the local leader in the following specialties: Excavation, Landscape Supplies and Septic.
Services include Pool digging or filling, driveway removal, basement waterproofing, ponds dug or filled, gardens, cisterns, septic tanks, sewers, basement walkouts, demolition, underground utilities, rock breaking and removal, hauling.

Contact Information

Web Address
https://ligonexcavation.com/
Face Book URL
https://www.facebook.com/Ligon-Excavation-Inc-2240073616077689/
Appointments:ligonexcavation.com
Email:ligon@commspeed.net
Telephone # 928-300-2126
Telephone # 928-567-8537

Camp Verde Business-HWY 260 West of I-17

√ Out of Africa

3505 W. State Route 260
DRIVE-THRU TOURS ARE OPEN!
This is your opportunity to get out of the house
and help support the animals and keepers who
make it possible. 930A-5P Daily (regular hours)

Contact Information

Web Address
https://outofafricapark.com/
Face Book URL
https://www.facebook.com/OutOfAfricaPark
Email: ashton@outofafricapark.com
Telephone # 928-567-2840

P & C Electric

Camp Verde, AZ
Owned and operated by Paul Pomeroy, with
over 30 years of experience in the trade P & C
Electric LLC is here to help you with all your
electrical needs, big or small. Paul got started in
the electrical trade in 1983, right after graduating
from high school. During his apprenticeship
years, he had the opportunity to learn the trade
from multiple master electricians allowing him
to perfect his abilities and skills. Paul got his
electrical contracting license in 1989, and with
that began his journey, helping homeowners and
business owners alike.
Areas served: Camp Verde and nearby area

Contact Information
Telephone # 928-300-9592

Rancho Verde RV Park LLC

1488 W Horseshoe Bend
Camp Verde, AZ 86322
Rancho Verde RV Park is a Boutique Adult
Oriented Park located in the beautiful Verde
Valley in a quiet residential neighborhood, a short
distance to Sedona, Jerome, Cottonwood, Prescott,
and Flagstaff.The park has mature shade trees,
gravel pads some with concrete patios, grass areas,
a seasonal creek and dog park. Complimentary
WiFi available throughout the park. Dark Sky
Community. Family owned and operated.

Contact Information

Web Address
http://ranchoverdervpark.com/
Face Book URL
https://www.facebook.com/ranchoverdervpark
Email: info@ranchopark.com
Telephone # 928-567-7037

Safetree PPE

Camp Verde-home based business
Lucas Renfroe. Assisting local businesses and
government entities safely reopen with quality
PPE at competitive pricing. Offering all forms
of PPE: various kinds of gloves, masks, gowns,
thermometers etc.

Contact Information
Email: Luke@safetreeppe.com
Telephone # 928-224-8507

Southwest Tank And Steel, Inc.

4900 N Hayfield Draw
Camp Verde, AZ 86322
Southwest Tank and Steel provides quality
products and services for design, new
construction, repair, painting and inspection
of aboveground storage tanks (AST's).
Southwest Tank and Steel services include new
construction, inspection, repair, and retrofit of
above ground storage tanks. We also have the
technical expertise to provide turnkey services
for all your AWWA and API tank needs.

Contact Information

Web Address
https://www.southwesttank.com/services/
Face Book URL
https://www.facebook.com/
SouthwestTankAndSteelInc
Email: rich@southwesttank.com
Telephone # 928-646-5900

The Verde DriveIn

The Verde Drive In will unfortunately be pausing
movie theater operations for the time being, as our
founder is a member of the Armed Services and is
being called into duty. Look for it to open back up
soon!

Contact Information

Web Address
https://www.verdedrivein.com/
Face Book URL
https://www.facebook.com/VerdeDriveIn/
Email: dave@verdedrivein.com

√ Verde Ranch Car and RV Wash

1896 W. Moonrise Dr.
Camp Verde Az, 86322
Brand new, automated, state-of-the-art, touch
free and soft touch wash systems

• Extra large bays for| RV's and 5th Wheels
Drying towels
Free vacuum stations
Wash, Wax, Detail, Claybar, Headlight
Restoration
SI02 & 9H Ceramic Coatings for 12, 24 and
36 Month Protection

Open 24 hours a day
Attendant on Duty;
Mon 8:00am - 8:00pm
Tue 8:00am - 8:00pm
Wed 8:00am - 8:00pm
Thur 8:00am - 8:00pm
Fri 8:00am - 8:00pm

Web Address
https://www.carandrvwash.com

√ Verde Ranch RV Resort

1105 Dreamcatcher Drive
We're conveniently located right off of the
highway and near many great local attractions and
businesses. Work from anywhere with our high-
speed WiFi. Relax and unwind by our pool, let the
kids play in the splash pad, or the dogs run in our
spacious dog park! Looking for adventure? Take
advantage of our river access, hike the nearby
trails, kayak the river or take a day trip to Sedona,
Prescott, or Cottonwood from our RV Resort,
to experience everything Arizona has to offer.

Contact Information

Web Address
https://verderanchrvresort.com/
Face Book URL
https://www.facebook.com/verderanchrvresort/
Email: vrrvinfo@crrmgmt.com
Telephone # 928-517-5310

Camp Verde Business-HWY 260 West of I-17

Verde River RV Resort

Address:1472 W Horseshoe Bend
Camp Verde, AZ 86322
Quiet and serene, nestled in the Verde Valley
we offer full amenities and the most magnificent
desert and mountain vistas you can imagine.
Workout in our state of the art Fitness Center
and relax by the over sized fire place inside the
newly remodeled Clubhouse or take a dip in our
huge heated pool.

AMENITIES:
Large heated pool with beautiful mountain
views and perfect for volleyball and aerobics
- 1 Large Spa with 20 powerful jets
- Fishing, canoes, paddleboards, and kayaking
- Club house and lounge ideal for reunions
  and weddings
- Fitness Center with treadmills, ellipticals,
  bikes, free & cable weights, and stretch
  matts
- Billiard Room with two Oldhausen
  professional tables
- Arts & Crafts for unique kid activities from
  ceramic painting to tie dye t-shirts
- Resort Center for check-in and store with
  the basics as well as unique local treasures
- Leash free dog park
- Lighted Pickleball Courts

Contact Information
Web Address
https://verderiverrvresort.com/
Face Book URL
https://www.facebook.com/
horseshoebenddrcampverde
Email: verderiverrv@gmail.com
Telephone # 928-202-3409

____

Verde Valley Auto Glass

2095 W. Horseshoe Bend Dr.
Next day service is available and we offer free
mobile service for Camp Verde, Cottonwood,
and Sedona areas. City Lic #3410 State Lic
#21189677.

- Luxury Car Windshield Replacement
- Foreign & Domestic Windshield Replacement
- Exotic Import Windshield Replacement
- Trucks

8A-5P 7 days a week
Contact Information
Web Address
https://www.vvautoglass.com/
Face Book URL
https://www.facebook.com/howell2988/
Email: verdevalleyautoglass@yahoo.com
Telephone # 928-963-4321

____

West Direct Oil

4850 N Hayfield Draw Dr, Camp Verde, AZ 86322
Lubricants & Ancillary Products. West Direct Oil
is ready to supply you with the premium lubricants
and ancillary products needed to meet your
business needs. Let us be your one stop shop for
bulk products and packaged goods.
Hours: Open 24 hours
Contact Information
Web Address
https://www.westdirectoil.com/
Email: Not Available
Telephone # 928-567-3346

____

WD's Auto-Motives LLC

Address:4700 Hayfield Draw Dr
Camp Verde, AZ 86322
Auto repair shop
Contact Information
Telephone # 928-821-3824

Yavapai-Apache Sand & Rock

3750 Old Hwy 279
Ready Mix Concrete supplier. Custom colored concrete, pouring concrete.
Summer 6A-3P Mon-Thur, 6A-2P Friday
Winter 7A-4P Mon-Thur, 7A-3P Friday
Contact Information
Web Address
https://www.yasr.co/
Face Book URL
https://www.facebook.com/yavapai.apache.sand.rock
Email: yasr@commspeed.net
Telephone # 928-567-3109

Yavapai Fence

4560 W. Old Corral Lane
Custom fencing, electric gate installation and maintenance, private fencing, arena fencing, ornamental fencing, chain link, equestrian pipe fencing, corral fencing. M-F 7A-3:30
Contact Information
Web Address
http://www.yavapaifence.com/
Telephone # 928-634-4950

Zuks Off Road

4900 N Hayfield Draw Dr Building C, Camp Verde, AZ 86322
We are still a family owned custom fabrication and product manufacturer shop dedicated to Suzuki and Toyota 4x4s.
Contact Information
Web Address
http://www.zuksoffroad.com/
Email: Not Available
Telephone # 928-567-3061

→Rimrock

America Tax

3095 E. Beaver Creek Rd.
Taxes, accounting, bookkeeping, and notary. Spanish available. 10:30A-6P Mon-Thur, Sat and Wed 10:30-3P.
Contact Information
Web Address
https://www.myamericatax.com/
Face Book URL
https://www.facebook.com/americaaccounting/
E-Mail
ivana@myamericatax.com
Telephone # 928-221-3446

Anything Goes Feed and Tack

Dry Beaver Feed Store
2110 E. Beaver Creek Rd.
Quality Feed and Pet Food. We are pleased to present to you our full line of non-GMO poultry and livestock feed created to provide your domestic animals both outstanding health and productivity. Our non-GMO feed line is bursting with nutrients, being formulated with organic mineral supplements and locally grown grains. In a world where many of the feeds are medicated, normone laced, and genetically modified, Beaver Creeks' holistic feeds are a refreshment. If you have a pasture poultry operation, family farm, a small dairy, try using our top quality feeds. Always remember, "You are what they eat."
Contact Information
Telephone # 928-202-7120

Camp Verde Business-Rimrock

Ashley L. Pelletier

Licensed & Board Certified Massage Therapist
3325 Beaver Creek Rd. # 102
Wed-Sat 9A-4P, Sun-Mon Closed. Available by
appointment.
Contact Information
Web Address
https://ashley-l-pelletier-licensed-board-certified.
business.site/
Telephone # 928-227-1188

____

Beaver Creek Adult Center

4250 Zuni Way Rimrock, AZ
Welcome to the Beaver Creek Adult Center's
Website. The Beaver Creek Adult Center serves
the community with many fun and exciting events,
monthly, weekly and daily, Monday thru Friday.
Some of our activities include concerts, Yoga, Pot
Luck dinners, Pinochle & Bridge games, rummage
and clothing sales, and getting together for coffee.
We have a Lending Library for our members.

Please see our activity page for more information
and scheduling. We are a 501(c) (3) non-profit
corporation. All operations are done by volunteer
hosts and hostesses. Beaver Creek Adult Center is
for Beaver Creek area residents 21 years old and
up. Various community organizations such as the
Beaver Creek Community Association, formerly
(LMPOA) , Kiwanis, Beaver Creek Trails
Coalition, Beaver Creek Preservation & Historical
Society, Lake Montezuma Women's Civic Club,
and Friends of the Well hold meetings here. The
center may also be rented for meetings, group get
togethers, birthday parties etc. We are the proud
parent organization of Beaver Creek Transit, also
known affectionately as the Beaver Buggy.
Contact Information
Web Address
https://beavercreekadultcenter.com/
Face Book URL
https://www.facebook.com/1bcac
Email: bcac4556@gmail.com
Telephone # 928-567-4556

Beaver Creek Chiropractic

Dr. David B. Lehenbauer D.C CCSP
4220 East Zuni Way
Contact Information
Telephone # 928-567-0006   928-284-0004

____

Beaver Creek Gasmart

3675 Beaver Creek Rd. Rimrock
Gas and Convenience Store, Water Dispensary
5A-10P Daily
Contact Information
Face Book URL
https://www.facebook.com/Beaver-Creek-Gas-
Mart-544911945548864/
Email: beavercreekgasmart@gmail.com
Telephone # 928-592-0300

____

Beaver Creek Inn

422 N. Montezuma Ave, Rimrock AZ
Welcome to our family-run rural village style
inn off the beaten path in picturesque Lake
Montezuma. This hidden gem community just
south of Sedona offers value-laden lodging to
those traveling for business, pleasure or catching
up with family and friends. The Inn's 22
room Southwestern decor mixed with genuine
hospitality combines the comforts of home with
hotel conveniences.
Contact Information
Web Address
https://beavercreekinnaz.com/
Face Book URL
https://www.facebook.com/
BeaverCreekInnRimrock/
Email: info@beavercreekinnaz.com
Telephone # 928-567-4475

____

Beaver Creek Liquor Store

3675 East Beaver Creek Rd. Rimrock
8A-10P Sun-Thur, 8A-11P Fri-Sat
Contact Information
Telephone # 928-592-0300

Beaver Creek Realty

3325 Beaver Creek Rd. #101
Debra Riley Broker
Featuring Lake Montezuma, Rimrock, Cornville,
Camp Verde, Cottonwood, Clarkdale, Jerome and
Sedona. Free Maps
Contact Information
Web Address
https://www.beavercreekrealty.com/
Face Book URL
https://www.facebook.com/beavercreekrealty
Email: deb@beavercreekrealty.com
Email: beavercreekrealty@gmail.com
Telephone # 928-567-7448

Beaver Creek Self Storage

Location of Storage: 3475 E. Beaver Creek Rd.
Rimrock, AZ
Management Offices: Beaver Creek Realty
3325 E. Beaver Creek Rd. Rimrock
Payments: Check, Cash, Credit Cards. We have
been in business for over 25 years in Rimrock
Arizona. Our facilities are well kept, well-lighted
and secured with key-pad access. Office Hours:
Monday thru Friday 9 a.m. to 5 p.m, Saturday 10
a.m. to 3 p.m, Sunday – Closed. Security Gate
Hours 7 a.m. to 7 p.m. Monday thru Sunday.
Contact Information
Web Address
http://www.beavercreekselfstorage.net/
Email: debr149@gmail.com
Telephone #
Phone: 928-567-7448
Fax: 928-567-7449

Beaver Creek Service Center

Napa Auto Care Center
3718 East Beaver Creek Rd, Rimrock
Our business takes quality and customer service
seriously. As a NAPA AutoCare Center, we follow
a strict Code of Ethics so customers will know
upfront what to expect. We Perform high-quality
diagnostic and repair services at a fair price, using
quality NAPA parts. Hours M-F 8A-5P
Contact Information
Web Address
https://www.napaonline.com/en/
autocare/?facilityId=53184
Face Book URL
https://www.facebook.com/Beaver-Creek-Service-
Center-377103375693729/
Email: dufresnebus@msn.com
Telephone #
Office: 928-567-5652
Tow: 520-699-2122
Fax: 520-567-0125

Beaver Creek Traders

3450 East Beavercreek Rd., Rimrock
Rim Rocks, crystals, minerals, specimens, jewelry,
ceramics, antiques, collectibles, vinyl records,
watch and jewelry repair. Buy, sell, trade.
Contact Information
Face Book URL
https://www.facebook.com/BeavercreekTradersAZ
Telephone # 928-846-8290 928-301-5411

Brewer Excavating LLC

Mailing: PO Box 1198, Rimrock, Az 85335
With over 18 years of experience, we are proudly serving the Verde Valley and the surrounding areas. At Brewer Excavating, customer satisfaction is our number one priority! We are not finished until you are pleased, and the job is complete. Give us a call for a free estimate. We look forward to working with you. We have worked on, from small septic installations to major grading projects.

Contact Information

Web Address
https://brewerexcavating.com/
Face Book URL
https://www.facebook.com/BrewerExcavating/about
Email: brewertravis1@gmail.com
Telephone # 928-300-4659

Candy's Creekside Cottage Antiques & Collectibles

2130 E. Beaver Creek Rd.
Antique Store, gift shop, Thrift Store and Consignment Store. Pistols and Petticoats. Old-time portrait parlor. 11A-5P Mon-Fri

Contact Information

Face Book URL
https://www.facebook.com/candyscreeksidecottage/
Email: candyscreeksidecottage@yahoo.com
Telephone # 602-402-9075

Canyon Medical Clinic

4200 East Zuni Way
Walk-in Medical Clinic
Family Practice, Immediate Services, No Appointment Needed, Flexibility.
Tue-Fri, Sat 8A-12P, Thur 1P-5P, Open 1st and 3rdSaturday only. Closed Sunday.

Contact Information

Web Address
https://canyon-med.com/
Face Book URL
https://www.facebook.com/campverdechamber
Email: canyon-med@canyon-med.com
Telephone #
Rimrock 928-592-9424
Black Canyon City 623-0374-5070
Glendale 623-374-5070

Car & Cycle Seat Upholstery

3325 Beaver Creek Rd #106, Rimrock.
Repair or completely replace car and motorcycle seat upholstery, add or replace leather steering wheel covers, furniture. If you urgently need to repair one seat, you can bring a car or motorcycle in the evening after work and pick up in the morning. Mon 2P-6P, Tu-Thu 10A-6P, Sat 10A-2P

Contact Information

Web Address
https://carcycle-seat-upholstery.business.site/
Face Book URL
https://www.facebook.com/Car-and-motorcycle-seat-upholstery-1690466197655278/
Email: snowflake1anna@gmail.com
Telephone # 928-821-5562

Reserved add space for Chamber adds.

Call to reserve space. Must be a member.

1/4 Page $100, 1/2 Page $200, Full Page $400

Camp Verde Business-Rimrock

DETECTRONICS

Commercial & residential. Installation, service and monitoring of intrusion, access control, fire, co, temperature, water damage, power supervision and standby generators.

Contact Information

Web Address

https://detectronics.com/

Face Book URL

https://www.facebook.com/campverdechamber

Telephone # 928-567-5599

Dollar General

3255 E. Beaver Creek Rd.
Bargain retail chain selling a range of household goods, groceries, beauty products & more.
8A-9P 7 days a week

Contact Information

Web Address

https://www.dollargeneral.com/

Telephone # 480-712-4038

Emerald Waves Healing and Treasure Chest Health Spa

3470 E. Beaver Creek Rd. Rimrock
The serenity you seek in a Yoga Studio, The fun you seek in fitness and dance classes, the wellness and healing you expect from massage and reiki. Plus beautiful gifts, tarot, objects 'd art in an affordable, comfortable and personal atmosphere. Located in quaint Rimrock, minutes from Camp Verde, Cornville, and Sedona.

Contact Information

Web Address

http://emeraldwaveshealing.com/

Face Book URL

https://www.facebook.com/Emerald-Waves-Healing-Treasure-ChestEmerald-Waves-Soulutions-591668727851889/

Email: emeraldwaveshealing@yahoo.com

Telephone # 928-438-9283

Family Dollar

3125 E. Beaver Creek Rd.
Your neighborhood Family Dollar store has low prices on a wide assortment of items, including cleaning supplies, discount groceries, and seasonal items and toys. You'll also find great deals on kitchen essentials, laundry supplies, and food and beverages, including the basics like milk, eggs, and bread. Plus, you can use your Family Dollar app and easily clip Smart Coupons – our exclusive digital coupons – for even greater savings on your next shopping trip. 8A-8P daily

Contact Information

Web Address

https://www.familydollar.com/locations/az/lake-montezuma/26880/

Telephone # 928-325-6122

Fiscor Heating and Cooling

3325 Beaver Creek Rd. # 103
M-F 7A-4P If not in office, please call.

Contact Information

Web Address

https://fiscorhvac.com/

Telephone # 928-300-4002

Harvey's Roofing LLC

3325 E Beaver Creek Rd #106, Rimrock, AZ
86335
Our customers are primarily homeowners
throughout Northern Arizona. We believe that we
offer exceptional value in our workmanship and in
the products we provide. Our Arizona Contractors
License number is 318928 and can be seen AZ
ROC License. Family owned and operated by
Michael Harvey, Harvey Roofing LLC has built its
reputation by doing things right.
For over 20 years, we have stood behind our
work. All of the materials we use are installed
as per the manufacturers specifications and
recommendations. The work we do is in
accordance with all Building Codes and
Regulations. Harvey's Roofing LLC can provide
warranties and will honor all written guarantees.
Our team is set up for EMERGENCY REPAIRS,
entire re-roofs, and small projects like mobile
home roofs and porch roofs. We can provide
a Free Estimate for a roof inspection and offer
options on materials, products, and colors

Contact Information

Web Address

https://harveysroofingllc.com/
Face Book URL
https://www.facebook.com/Harveysroofingllc/
Email: harveysroofingllc.com
Email: mike.harvey95@gmail.com
Telephone # 928-301-9015

____

Heartlinks Woodworks

2110 E. Beaver Creek Rd.
Locally made wood items. Custom inlay cutting
boards, lazy Susan's, Folding tables, custom
veneering, Petrified wood and petrified wood
items, Natural Turquoise pieces. 10A-6P Mon-Fri
Contact Information
Face Book URL
https://www.facebook.com/
heartlinkswoodworksllc/
Email: heartlinkswoodworksllc@gmail.com
Telephone # 928-301-1101

____

Jim's Trading Post

2115 East Beaver Creek Rd. Mcguireville
Antiques, collectibles, unusual, buy, sell, trade.
Fine art, fine junk, and fine folk. 10A-5P Daily.
Contact Information
Face Book URL
https://www.facebook.com/jimstradingpost/
Email: jimandrus@gmail.com
Telephone # 928-554-5526

____

√ Kiwanis International Clothes Closet

3095 E. Beaver Creek Rd.
Resale Clothing & Accessories with a target for
children's clothes. Tu-Thur 10A-3P, Sat 10A-3P
Contact Information
Face Book URL
https://www.facebook.com/Kiwanis-Clothes-
Closet-1847422331954507/
Email: econn133@gmail.com
Telephone # 928-300-2640 928-300-6072

____

Camp Verde Business-Rimrock

Magnolia Beauty Bar

3325 Beaver Creek Rd. #105

Kirsti is an artist when it comes to blonding, coloring and styling. Her education includes several advanced blonding classes, extension certifications, and quarterly knowledge in all upcoming techniques. Services include haircuts, blow dry, coloring, highlights, balayage, fantasy colors, olaplex, waxing and eyelash extensions by Emily H.   M-F 9A-4P Sat by appointment

Contact Information

Web Address

https://magnoliabeautybars.com/

Face Book URL

https://www.facebook.com/magnoliabeautybar

Email: magnoliarimrock@gmail.com

Telephone #

928-821-0256 for all Hair Services

928-301-4528 for Eyelash Extensions

____

McGuireville Minimart

2105 E. Beaver Creek, McGuireville

Gas, ATM, Convenience Store

____

Montezuma Appliance Repair

3095 E. Beaver Creek Rd.

We specialize in appliance repair and in home services for major appliance brands. We service the Verde Valley, Sedona, Flagstaff, and Prescott areas. Our service fee is a competitive.

Mon: 9:30 AM – 2:00 PM, Tue-Fri: 9:30 AM – 4:00 PM. Sat/Sun: Closed

Contact Information

Web Address

https://montezuma-appliance-repair.com/

Email: MontezumaApplianceRepair@gmail.com

Telephone # 928-592-9382

Montezuma Family Dental

Kyle Carter DDS

4283 N. Pima Way, Lake Montezuma

Dr. Kyle Carter would like to thank you for stopping by. We are a full service dental practice for both children and adults which includes cosmetic and restorative dentistry. Establishing and maintaining the highest degree of oral health is the top priority for our patients. Montezuma Family Dentistry can improve your smile from simple whitening procedures to complete dental make overs. We accept almost all insurances, including AHCCCS. No insurance? No problem. Ask about our in-house dental plan. Exams, x-rays, dentures, root canals. 8A-5P

Contact Information

Web Address

https://montezumadental.com/

Face Book URL

https://www.facebook.com/Montezuma-Family-Dental-1622879047989141/

Email: montezumadental@gmail.com

Telephone # 928-202-4787

____

Northern Arizona Pump Inc.

5325 N. Restoration Loop Rimrock AZ
Nathan (Nate) White, owner, and operator started
Northern Arizona Pump in 1977 with a Mountain
Bell A-frame and $6.00 in his bank account. Today
we have 3 drill rigs, 3 pump trucks, and 2 service
trucks. We offer complete service and installation
of Commercial, Residential, and Irrigator
Water Wells. Additional Services offered are as
follows: Well Inspections, Water Quality Testing,
Constant Pressure Systems, Complete Well Pump,
Equipment Service, Well Equipment Repair,
New Well Drilling – Cable & Tool Rotary, Well
Deepening, Well Clean Outs, Well Abandonment,
Storage Tanks, Sediment/Sand Filter Systems,
Pressure/Expansion Tanks, Well Video, Solar
Pump Systems, Annual Well Maintenance and
Inspections, Windmills. Monday - Thursday: 8am
- 4pm Friday: 8am-2pm
Contact Information
Web Address
https://norazpump.com/
Face Book URL
https://www.facebook.com/northernarizonapump
Email: office@norazpump.com
Telephone # 928-634-4978

Petmec Plumbing Solutions

3920 E Millennium Way, Rimrock, AZ, 86335
Petmec Plumbing Solutions/Pettijohn Mechanical
Inc.
We have been serving the entire Verde Valley
for over 30yrs. Fast, friendly affordable service
is what we are all about. From new construction
to minor repairs, let us handle all your plumbing
needs. If water runs through it we do it! We are
Pettijohn Mechanical doing business as Petmec
Plumbing Solutions.
The coordinates that you can use in navigation
applications to get to find "Petmec Plumbing
Solutions/Pettijohn Mechanical Inc." quickly are
34.655380249023,-111.78199005127
Plumbing, Plumber, Plumbing Repair, Plumbing
contractor, Water Heater
Contact Information
Face Book URL
https://www.facebook.com/Petmec-Plumbing-
Solutions-390743647662960/
Email: Not Available
Telephone # 928-567-3092

Rask Construction

3174 E Beaver Creek Rd, Rimrock, AZ 86335
Mail: PO Box 387, Camp Verde, AZ 86322
General building construction
Contact Information
Telephone # 928-567-3203

Rimrock Resale Shoppe

3275 E. Beaver Creek Rd. Rimrock AZ
New and Used items
9A-4P Daily
Telephone # 928-567-4272

Camp Verde Business-Rimrock

Robbies
5155 N. Dave Wingfield Rd. Rimrock
Burgers, cold beer, pizza
Take Out, Dine-In, Outside Dining
11A-8P Daily
Contact Information
Face Book URL
https://www.facebook.com/RobbiesRestaurantAZ/
Email: robbiesrimrock@yahoo.com
Telephone # 928-592-9171

———————

Rimrock Super Storage
3700 E. Beaver Creek Rd. Rimrock
Only two miles off I-17 from Exit 293 at 3706 East
Beaver Creek Road across from the Post Office.
Access 7 days a week. On-Site Management.
Friendly Hometown Atmosphere. We accept Visa,
Mastercard, Discover, Visa Debit Cards and Auto
Bill Pay. Office Hours M-F 10A-5P, Security Gate
Hours 6A-8P Daily.
Contact Information
Web Address
http://rimrockstorage.com/index.htm
Email: rimrockstorage@qwestoffice.net
Telephone # 928-567-5005

———————

Small Engine Repair
3095 E. Beaver Creek Rd.
Echo—the Prop Performance
Contact Information
Telephone # 928-567-2267

Thai Garden
3460 E. Beaver Creek Rd. Rimrock
Thai Food. Dine-in, Take-out
Tues-Sun 11A-8:30P
Contact Information
Web Address
www.thaigardenrimrock.com
Telephone # 928-592-9117
928-254-9736

———————

The Fitzgerald Company Building and Design LLC
3325 Beaver Creek Rd. # 104
New construction to remodel, residential and
commercial. 7A-5P M-F Call for Appointment.
Contact Information
Telephone # 928-451-6519

———————

Two Feathers Healing Arts
4230 East Zuni Way, Lake Montezuma
Diana Toltz LMT
Massage. M-Sat by Appointment
Contact Information
Telephone # 928-202-0316

———————

→Surrounding Areas

Advance Cleaning Technologies

Camp Verde Az 86322

Have your floors seen better days? Let us at Advanced Cleaning Technologies A-Z, LLC solve your carpet and tile frustrations today with a deep and thorough cleaning. Family owned and operated business serving Sedona, Prescott, Flagstaff, and Northern Arizona regions. You can trust us to remove unsightly stains and restore the look of your tile or carpeted floors with in-depth tile, floor, and carpet cleaning services.

Contact Information

Web Address

https:// https://cleaningaz.com/

Face Book URL

https://www.facebook.com/
Advancedcleaningtechnologies/

Telephone # 928-300-7452

A.L.D. Development. Inc

Verde Valley Dirt Work and Hauling –
Camp Verde, AZ 86322

Specializing in residential and commercial projects. A.L.D. Inc. is a family owned and operated company that has been in business since 1996. The dirt business started when I got my first real tractor. I couldn't find enough dirt to move on our property so I started doing work for my neighbors. This soon grew and before long I was doing it for other people. As time went on I got licensed and insured. Now I own six different tractors and a large dump truck for hauling, and am always looking for more equipment to better serve my customers.

Contact Information

Web Address

https://www.vvdirtwork.com

Email: Mparja89@gmail.com

Telephone # 928-300-4578

APS

6672 Corsair Ave. Prescott

Contact Information

Web Address

https://www.aps.com/en/residential/home

Telephone # 928-443-6614

Camp Verde Business-Surrounding Areas

Arizona Community Foundation of Sedona

P.O. Box 558
Founded in 1991 as the Greater Sedona Community Foundation, the Arizona Community Foundation of Sedona secures, manages, and allocates donor gifts for charitable purposes in Sedona and the Verde Valley, working to improve the quality of life for all residents.

Contact Information

Web Address
https://www.azfoundation.org/Give-Where-You-Live/Sedona
Face Book URL
https://www.facebook.com/AZFoundation
Email: tmcconnell@azfoundation.org
Telephone # 928-339-7218

√ Arizona Rangers

Verde Valley Company #17
Mailing Address;
Verde Valley Company
Arizona Rangers
P.O. Box 1109
Sedona, Az. 86339
Few but proud, then and now. Established in 1901
Law enforcement assistance and security services.
Supporting youth programs. Mounted Unit.

Contact Information

Web Address
http://vvrangers.org/index.asp.html
Face Book URL
https://www.facebook.com/vvrangers
Email: verdevalley.info@azrangers.gov
Telephone # 928-339-7218

Black Bear Enterprises LLC

Camp Verde, AZ
Is a gun and firearm FFL Dealer in Camp Verde AZ 86322. You can buy or pickup your firearm from this location. BLACK BEAR ENTERPRISES LLC | Firearm Dealer and FFL Store in Camp Verde AZ 86322

Contact Information

Web Address
https://www.fflapi.com/store/black-bear-enterprises-llc/
Email: Not Available
Telephone # 505-321-1055

Blevins Backhoe Service

Camp Verde, AZ
Septic tank contractor. We provide water main repair, septic tank installation, backflow preventer installation and other services.
Bart Blevins Backhoe Service. Septic Tank Service - Cottonwood, AZ. Projects, photos, reviews and more | Porch

Contact Information
Email: Not Available
Telephone # 928-567-6529

Bryson Ranch LLC

Camp Verde, AZ
A freight shipping Trucking Company, Transportation Services provided: Flatbed

Contact Information

Web Address
http://www.truckcompaniesin.com/dot/3199826/
Email: Not Available
Telephone # 928-300-9817

Build It Brothers Construction

2221 E. Sierra Verde Rd 59, Camp Verde Az 86322

Local, family owned and operated, Build It Brothers Construction offers Stucco repairs, Interior and exterior painting, Pressure washing, Landscaping & debris removal, Hauling, Bathroom repairs, Gutter cleaning, and Roof repair.

Contact Information

Web Address

https://visitcampverde.com/campverde/build-it-brothers-construction/

Telephone # 928-379-9397

Camp Verde Plumbing

Camp Verde, AZ 86322

Water Heater, Septic, Leaks, drain cleaning, remodel.

Hours: Open 24 hours

Contact Information

Web Address

https://campverdeplumbing.com/

Face Book URL

https://www.facebook.com/campverdeplumbing/

Email: info@campverdeplumbing.com

Email: josh@campverdeplumbing.com

Telephone # 844-287-5862

√ Cornville Historical Society

P.O. Box 1200

Cornville, AZ 86325

The mission of the Cornville Historical Society is to gather, preserve and share information about the history of the Cornville-Page Springs area from the time of pioneer settlement in the 1870's to the present. The Society does research, keeps records, collects historical items, and sponsors educational activities relating to rural life in the historic Lower Oak Creek area.

Contact Information

Web Address

https://www.cornville-historical-society.org/

Email: info@cornville-historical-society.org

Telephone # 928 649-1426 (Janet Cassagio)

Dana Windes/Rink Windes Wood Floors LLC

Camp Verde, AZ

Rick Windes Wood Floors is family owned and operated. We've been serving the Flagstaff and Sedona area for 25 years. Rick is a licensed contractor, bonded and insured. Outstanding with customers.

Contact Information

Web Address

https://www.bizapedia.com/people/arizona/camp-verde/dana-windes.html

Email: Not Available

Telephone # 928-606-2469

Camp Verde Business-Surrounding Areas

David Mathews Outfitters

P.O. Box 4417
Camp Verde, AZ 86322
David Mathews Outfitters specializes in all western big game trophy animals. We offer one on one archery, Rifle and muzzle loader hunts in Arizona and New Mexico for the following species, Elk, Mule Deer, Antelope, Coues Deer, Oryx, Ibex and Big Horn Sheep. We also offer pre-season scouting trips. David Mathews Outfitters is owned and operated by David Mathews or "Davey" as most people in the hunting industry know him by. He is an outdoor fanatic that enjoys taking people hunting with one goal in mind, harvest the biggest critters in the woods! We are a true trophy outfitter, and we strive to please everyone. We provide quality one on one hunts with experienced guides who know the animals and the territory.

Contact Information
Web Address
http://www.davidmathewsoutfitters.com/
Face Book URL
https://www.facebook.com/davidmathewsoutfitters
Email: dmoutfitters@hotmail.com
Telephone # 928-300-6405

Dianna's Place

Camp Verde, AZ
Hair dresser
Contact Information
Telephone # 928-567-5270

Dickison Pump & Well Drilling

Camp Verde, AZ
Water Well Services, pressure Tanks and Pump Installation , repair and Maintenance.
Contact Information
Face Book URL
https://www.facebook.com/Dickison-Pump-And-Well-105242951124040/?ref=page_internal
Email: debbie86322@yahoo.com
Telephone # 928-567-3538

Digital Ease LLC

Camp Verde, AZ 86322
Digital Ease LLC, has been serving Northern Arizona with professional, on-site installation and service of a variety of technology products for over a decade. We design custom systems with the mindset that a simple, easy-to-use system will get used more often.

Our key services include:
- Distributed Audio & Video
- Security and Surveillance systems
- Wireless and Wired Networks
- Control and Automation
- Structured Wiring for Home and
- Office Problem Solving

Proud to be a Licensed, Bonded and Insured low-voltage contractor.
ROC 274839
Website: https://www.digitaleasellc.com/
Contact Information
Web Address
https://www.digitaleasellc.com/
Email: cvcbacampverde@gmail.com
Telephone # 928-593-0120

DNR Freeze Dry LLC

Camp Verde, AZ

In the state of Arizona under the Food Cottage Program I sale freeze dried candies. I take your favorite candy from being hard, chewy, and sticky to airy, puffy, and with a more intense flavor in every bite! With melt in mouth goodness!

Contact Information

Face Book URL

https://www.facebook.com/dnrfreezedry/about/?ref=page_internal

Email: dnrfreezedry@gmail.com

Telephone # 928-203-6863

El Eden Landscaping

Camp Verde, AZ

We are a gardening
 company with the best prices. We guarantee our work because your satisfaction is our satisfaction.

Contact Information

Web Address

https://officaleledenlands.wixsite.com/eledenlandscaping

Face Book URL

https://www.facebook.com/eledenlandscaping/

Email: none listed

Telephone # 786-709-3057

Elite Performance Concrete

460 West Grippen Lane
Camp Verde, AZ 86322
Commercial Concrete Contractor
serving Sedona AZ and the entire Verde Valley.|Commercial-ConcreteElite Performance Concrete (EPC)is a full service concrete placement contractor. We provide Commercial concrete installation, residential concrete, and decorative concrete installations, specializing in placing and finishing concrete slabs, concrete restoration, concrete pouring.

Elite Performance Concrete Services:

- Commercial concrete installation
- Concrete polishing
- Concrete staining
- Concrete resurfacing
- Concrete resurfacing
- Decorative concrete floors

Contact Information

Web Address

http://www.eliteperformanceconcrete.com/

Email: coby@eliteperformanceconcrete.com

Telephone # (928) 821-0793

FAX 928-567-7709

√ Essential Massage

Heather Burton

Contact Information

Email: heatherbarton2014@gmail.com

Telephone # 541-253-1961

Camp Verde Business-Surrounding Areas

Evergreen Groomery

Camp Verde, AZ

Treat your furry family member to a gentle spa day. Whether it be just a bath, a deshed treatment, or the full spa works!! I specialize in breed specific cuts, poodles, and doodles! Evergreen Groomery is a gentle, calming dog salon.

Contact Information

Face Book URL

https://www.facebook.com/evergreengroomery

Email: Not Available

Telephone # 928-300-4312

Feldmeier Properties/Central AZ Consultants LLC

Bill Feldmeier

Contact Information

Email: bfeld@cableone.net

Franklin Pest Control

Camp Verde, AZ

Insects: Ants, Spiders, whether you've got bees, rodents, spiders (or you name it), we can assist with your pest problem. We can even provide same-day service. Drop us a line to schedule your pest control services today! Termites

Contact Information

Face Book URL

https://www.facebook.com/franklinpestcontrol/

Email: Not Available

Telephone # 928-202-6915

√ Fresh Focuses Photography

Mailing address;

469 Spruce, Camp Verde, Az 86322

If you've ever been to the Grand Canyon, Flagstaff, Prescott, Sedona or other beautiful sites in Northern Arizona, you are aware of the majesty of these areas. Now take your dream a step further and consider your next family portrait, wedding or even surprise proposal here. You will never forget that choice and Fresh Focuses Photography is sure to make sure you do not.

Contact Information

Web Address

https://freshfocuses.com/

Face Book URL

https://www.facebook.com/
FreshFocusesPhotography/

Telephone # 707-738-6369

√ Friends of the Verde River

115 S. Main Street, Suite B
Cottonwood, AZ 86326
Mailing address:
P. O. Box 2535, Cottonwood, AZ 86326
Friends of the Verde River (Friends) envisions a healthy, flowing Verde River and tributaries that support our natural environment, vibrant communities, and quality of life for future generations. We work collaboratively for a healthy, flowing Verde River system.

Contact Information

Web Address
https://verderiver.org/
Face Book URL
https://www.facebook.com/verderiverfriends/
Email: contactus@verderiver.org
Telephone # 928-641-6013

―――――――――

Full-Line Striping LLC

3581 N Smith Ave
Camp Verde, AZ 86322
Striping Solutions to Suit Durability Needs and Budgets Provided by Experts Nationally. Nationwide Installations.

We specialize in smaller jobs. We paint parking lots, curbing, handicap spaces, crosswalks, stop bars, etc. We have a $300 dollar minimum on smaller jobs.
Hours: Friday & Saturday 6AM-6PM

Contact Information

Web Address
https://campverdebiz.com/
Face Book URL
https://www.facebook.com/pages/category/
Product-Service/Full-Line-Striping-
LLC-112066310539632/
Email: jtfullmer.jf@gmail.com
Telephone # 928-592-3085

Grants Appliance Repair LLC

Camp Verde, AZ 86322
Services: Appliance Repair | Washer & Dryer Repair | Disposals | Refrigeration | Water Heaters
Hours: Monday-Friday 8:00-5:00

Contact Information

Web Address
https://www.grantsapplianceverdevalley.com/
Email: grantsappliance76@gmail.com
Telephone # 928-554-0900

―――――――――

Green River Hauling LLC

485 W Hereford Drive
Camp Verde, AZ 86322
Telephone # 928-300-0991

―――――――――

High Country Power Washing

Address: 1538 Boothill Drive
Camp Verde, AZ 86322
We are Northern Arizona's power washing experts. From your sidewalks to your equipment, High Country can keep it looking better for longer!

Contact Information

Face Book URL
https://www.facebook.com/
HighCountryPowerWashingLLC
Telephone # 928-592-8632

―――――――――

Camp Verde Business-Surrounding Areas

Illegal Street Wear

Camp Verde, AZ 86322
Vendor of line of clothes.
Contact Information
Web Address
http://www.illegalstreetwear.com/
Face Book URL
https://www.facebook.com/illegalstreetwear/
Telephone # (928) 399-0128

____

Kathy Tryon Mary Kay Cosmetics

Camp Verde, AZ
As a Mary Kay Independent Sales Director, I teach you how to take care of your skin with Mary Kay Cosmetics. I sell Mary Kay skin care, body care, fragrances and color cosmetics.
Contact Information
Web Address
http://www.marykay.com/ktryon
Face Book URL
https://www.facebook.com/KathyTryonMaryKay/
Email: kathy_tryon1@yahoo.com
Telephone # 928-567-7535

____

KM Drilling Inc

2432 Private Drive
Camp Verde, AZ 86322
PO Box 1738 Camp Verde, AZ 86322
Residential and Commercial Drilling Services.
*Water Wells *Geothermal *Exploration*Core Drilling *Pump Service. Located in Camp Verde Serving Arizona, Colorado, and California.
EMERGENCY SERVICES AVAILABLE 24 Hours a Day, 7 Day a Week 365 Days a Year. Call 928-567-3633 For Immediate Help
Hours: Mon-Fri 8-5 MST, Sat-Sun: Closed
Phone:(928) 567-3633
Contact Information
Web Address
https://kmdrillinginc.com/
Telephone # 928-567-3633

Mario And Mario Landscaping

Camp Verde, AZ 86322
Mario and Mario's Landscaping is an all-inclusive full landscaping/full masonry company that offers many different services that might benefit you and your needs. Some of the many services that Mario and Mario's Landscaping offers include lawn care service, full irrigation installation, and gardening services. All of these services are available in the Camp Verde, Cottonwood, and Flagstaff, Payson, Prescott and the greater Arizona area.
Hours: Mon- Saturday 08:00 Am - 5:00 Pm
Contact Information
Web Address
http://marioandmariolandscaping.com/
Face Book URL
https://www.facebook.com/Mario-and-Mario-Landscaping-567173886792369
Email: marioc483@aol.com
Telephone # 928-282-3118

____

MGG Cleaning Service

Camp Verde, AZ
If you require commercial cleaning or new construction cleaning services, our company has a solution for you. We also do residential & Airbnb property cleaning, move-in & move-out cleanup, deep cleaning, and medical clinic cleaning work. As one of the most flexible local residential and commercial cleaning companies, we also work in the areas: Lake Montezuma, AZ, Verde Village, AZ, Cottonwood, AZ, Village of Oak Creek, AZ, Clarkdale Town, AZ
If you have a residential or commercial property in Camp Verde, AZ and need general, deep, or construction cleanup services, our company is the perfect choice for you. Call us today to learn more!
Hours: 8-5 M-F
Contact Information
Web Address
https://mggcleaningservice.com/
Email: Not Available
Telephone # 928-378-7334

https://campverdebiz.com/   Camp Verde Chamber & Business Alliance

Camp Verde Business-Surrounding Areas

Msp Drywall LLC
Camp Verde, AZ 86322
Contact Information
Telephone # 623-581-0337

√ NACOG
Northern Arizona Council of Governments EWD

Services include Area on Aging, Head Start, Help with utilities, firewood, propane, Weatherization, economic/workplace development, home program CDBG, regional planning, Route 66 Browfield site revitalization.

Northern Arizona Council of Governments is a nonprofit corporation representing local governments to provide a wide variety of services within Apache, Coconino, Navajo and Yavapai Counties.

Solving common problems. Transcending geographical boundaries. Improving local communities. These are just a few of the tasks of the Northern Arizona Council of Governments (NACOG), a group of local governments representing Apache, Coconino, Navajo and Yavapai Counties. NACOG staff works with local governments to address similar issues faced by the communities within the region.

NACOG's Head Start Division provides comprehensive child development and family support services to economically disadvantaged children and their families.

NACOG's Human & Community Services Division is committed to the development of human and community services in areas ranging from supporting equal opportunities for persons with disabilities and delivering services to older individuals, to combating the conditions of poverty.

NACOG's Economic and Workforce Development Division helps build economic success through workforce development partnerships.

Comprehensive economic development planning for workforce, business services and tourism development is a major focus, as well as public works and infrastructure development for sustainable economic growth.

NACOG's Planning Division recognizes that studying area population and demographics is critical to planning a viable transportation system. NACOG provides these services to local governments, along with estimates and projections for population growth. The division also participates in regional transit planning activities, and coordinates with the Arizona Department of Transportation and local governments for transportation related funding. Additionally, the agency develops, adopts and maintains an area-wide water quality management plan.

Contact Information
Web Address
https://nacog.org/
https://yavapaiatwork.com
Email: lcickavage@nacog.org
clyons@nacog.org
Telephone # 928-774-1895

Camp Verde Business-Surrounding Areas

Nashwa Farms

Nashwa Farms Equine Boarding Facility & Hay Sales & Event Center for all types of events.
3500 W Mahoney Rd, Camp Verde, AZ 86322
Open for business - 7 days a week from 8 am to 5 pm for Hay Sales - Farm grown Alfalfa Hay, Bermuda Grass Hay, Wheat Hay, Tiff Hay, Rye Hay, Cow Hay, depending on the season.
Horse Boarding Facility offering full care boarding, Seasonal boarding either winter or summer, Retirement boarding for our favorite furry friends, vacation layovers we take care of your animals while your on vacation at our farm. Riding lessons are available.

* Special Events - Nashwa Farms offers ample room in our beautiful lush green pastures for small to larger groups for weddings, corporate events, fund raisers, clubs, non profit groups for fund raisers, music, photo shoots, we have lots of fun vintage farm equipment and trucks for pictures. Arena rentals for any type of event call for more information or a private tour of our facilities.
LOCAL FARM FAMILY owned & operated over 30 years - Historical farm established in 1876.

Contact Information

Web Address
https://nashwafarms.com/
Face Book URL
https://www.facebook.com/NashwaFarmsArena
Email: nashwamanager@gmail.com
Telephone # 602-695-8523

√ Sedona CanAm Rentals

2875 W State Rte 89A, Sedona, AZ 86336
We're currently offering 2021 CanAm Maverick X3 ATV Rentals that are available with 2 seats or 4 seats. Rental times range from 4 to 8 hours and pick up times are flexible. Helmets, goggles, maps of the trails, cooler, water and ice are all included with your ATV rental!

Contact Information

Web Address
https://www.sedonaslingshotrentals.com/
Face Book URL
https://www.facebook.com/sedonacanam
Email: sedonacanam@gmail.com
Telephone # 928-202-4126

Superior Exteriors Landscaping

Address: 1185 W Buffalo Trl Cv
Camp Verde, AZ 86322
Mailing: PO BOX 1040, Camp Verde, AZ 86322
Hardscaping, rock work, pavers, retaining walls and more.

Contact Information

Face Book URL
https://www.facebook.com/Superior-Exteriors-Landscape-Design-LLC-2037504643216588/
Email: superiorexteriorscv@gmail.com
Telephone # 928- 890-7202

TBL Investments

John Tewes
2519 Tolani Trail, Flagstaff
P.O. Box 22118
Contact Information
Email: myjob121@gmail.com
Telephone # 928-699-6780

____

TT's Batch Bakery

Bread & pastry the old-fashioned way: before
dawn, from scratch, using only the finest
ingredients, each piece carefully crafted by hand.
Contact Information
Web Address
https://www.ttsbatchbakery.com/
Email: Not Available
Telephone # 928-554-5336

____

That Ice Cream Cart

Camp Verde, AZ
Small ice cream cart servicing the local Camp
Verde neighborhoods. We are excited to sell ice
cream, soda, candy, chips, and popcorn
Contact Information
Face Book URL
https://www.facebook.com/
YellowTopCart/?ref=py_c
Email: thaticecreamcart@gmail.com

____

The Camp Verde Journal

Camp Verde, AZ
Local Newspaper
Contact Information
Web Address
https://www.journalaz.com/
Face Book URL
https://www.facebook.com/cottonwoodnews
Email: editor@larsonnewspapers.com
Telephone # 928-634-8551

√ Troap Holdings LLC

Jack McFarland
Contact Information
Email: jbmcorders@cox.net
Telephone # 928-382-7619

____

Verde Valley Internet LLC

Camp Verde, AZ
Verde Valley Internet is a WISP, a Wireless
Internet Service Provider.
A WISP doesn't need to bring wire to your
location, making it a good solution for serving
rural areas where telcos and cable companies
wouldn't invest. A WISP mounts antennas on
towers (or atop buildings) to transmit signal,
and will install a modem on the customer's
home or building to receive the wireless signal.
We are a locally owned and operated business,
established in 2018. We are dedicated to providing
a highspeed wireless point to point air fiber service
with:

* No Contracts
  No Data Allowances*
  No Slowing Based On Other Users' Activity
  Reliable Consistent Speeds
  All at competitive rates with minimal fees!

Contact Information
Web Address
https://www.vvinternet.com/
Email: info@vvinternet.com
Telephone # 928-567-9100

____

Camp Verde Business-Surrounding Areas

Unleashed Dog Training Az

Camp Verde, AZ 86322
Unleashed dog training website is here to help and be a support system for those clients whose dog I am working with. It's a place to get information on classes and a place to order training equipment. It will also offer a place you can get your questions answered in between training classes. It has a FYI section with free tips on some of the issues we are all faced with regarding our dogs.

Contact Information
Web Address
https://www.unleasheddogtrainingaz.com/
Telephone # 760-935-0521

Vortex ATV Rentals

551 N Main Street, Cottonwood
Family owned business. ATV rental with great prices. Two seaters, four seaters and six seaters.
Contact Information
Web Address
https://www.vortexatvrental.com/
Face Book URL
https://www.facebook.com/vortexatv/
Email: vortexatv@gmail.com
Telephone # 928-235-4520

Yaquis Taqueria

Camp Verde, AZ
Food Truck. Mexican food made with a lot of love, doesn't matter what you order Everything is delicious.
Contact Information
Face Book URL
https://www.facebook.com/Yaquis-Taqueria-1374900309457514/?ref=page_internal
Email: Not Available
Telephone # 928-300-2392

√ Yavapai College SBDC

Office locations: Clarkdale and Prescott Valley
Contact Information
Web Address https:// www.yc.edu/SBDC
REGISTER for Business Services
https://www.yc.edu/v6/small-business-development-center/
RECEIVE News and Upcoming Training Info
https://lp.constantcontactpages.com/su/bwwfdaH
Email: sbdc@yc.edu
Telephone # 928-717-7232

____

→Restaurants

Alfonsos

452 W Finnie Flat Rd. Suite E
Mexican Food
Take-out Drive Through Open 24 hr
Contact Information
Web Address
https://alfonsoscampverdeaz.com/
Face Book URL
https://www.facebook.com/pages/Alfonso's%20Mexican%20Food/978636698865523/
Email: familialuna1991@gmail.com
Telephone # 928-567-7296

____

Babe's Round Up

90 S. Montezuma Castle Hwy.
Mon-Sat 11A-9P Closed Sunday
Local BBQ. Pulled Pork, beef brisket, BBQ chicken with cowboy beans. Look for the smoker out front. Walk up window, Take Out, dine-in, outside seating.
Contact Information
Telephone # 928-567-6969
For catering 928-821-0205

https://campverdebiz.com/   Camp Verde Chamber & Business Alliance

Camp Verde Business-Restaurants

Beto's Corner

10 E. Cliff House Drive
7A-8P Mon-Fri 7A-2P Saturday. Closed Sunday
Take-out, drive-through window, eat-in
Contact Information
Web Address Recommendation
https://betoscorner.food62.com/
Face Book URL
https://www.facebook.com/pages/Beto's%20
Corner/109385769099709/
Telephone # 928-567-8897

Burger King

365 N. Goswick Way
6A-9P Mon-Sat, 7A-9P Sunday
Take-out, Drive Through window
Contact Information
Web Address
https://www.bk.com/
Face Book URL
https://www.facebook.com/burgerking
Telephone # 928-567-3401

Crusty's Pizza

522 W Finnie Flat Rd Ste A
Pizza, Italian Food
Hours 11am-8pm,
Take-out, eat in
Contact Information
Face Book URL
https://www.facebook.com/Crustys-
Pizza-125305074345684
Telephone # 928-567-6444

Dairy Queen

1580 W. State Route 260
Ice Cream, Fast Food
Drive Through Window, dine-in
Contact Information
Web Address
https://www.dairyqueen.com/en-us/
Face Book URL
https://www.facebook.com/dairyqueen
Telephone # 928-567-3229

Denny's

1630 West Arizona Hwy 260
All American Food
You can order ahead at Dennys.com or give us a
call at 9285679505
Hours are 7am-10pm. Kids Eat Free 7 Days a
week, all day long! 2 kid's meals for every 1 adult
entree purchased. Open for dine-in, take out, and
curbside pickup.
Contact Information
Web Address
https://www.dennys.com/order
Face Book URL
https://www.facebook.com/dennys/
Telephone # 928-567-9505

Camp Verde Business-Restaurants

Dominos

452 W Finnie Flat Rd
To order Pizza 9285540999
Take-out and delivery
DOMINO'S PIZZA & FOOD DELIVERY IN
CAMP VERDE, AZ
 Pizza, chicken, pasta, sandwiches, and more!
Domino's is the Camp Verde pizza restaurant
that delivers it all. Find a Domino's location near
you in Camp Verde and order your food online,
over the phone, or through the Domino's app for
delivery or carryout!
Hours: Sun-Thu: 10:30 am to 12:00 am, Fri: 10:30
am to 1:00 am, Sat: 10:30 am to 1:00 am

Contact Information

Web Address

https://pizza.dominos.com/arizona/camp-verde/
Telephone # 928-554-0999

—————————

El Patio Bar and Grill

1955 East Cornville Rd. Rimrock
Tex-Mex Restaurant 11A-8P Tues-Sun
Take Out, inside and outside Dining

Contact Information

Face Book URL

https://www.facebook.com/El-
patio-101943170140010/
Telephone # 928-592-0340

—————————

Filberto's

1650 W. State Route 260
Mexican Food
Drive Through Window Open 24 hr
Eat In dining, Take-out

Contact Information

Web Address

https://filibertos.com/
Face Book URL

https://www.facebook.com/FilibertosMexFood/
Telephone # 928-567-8754

—————————

Gabriela's

1580 W. State Route 260 Ste 2
Mexican Food
Monday - Thursday 7 A-4P, Friday -Sunday 7
A-8P
Drive Through Window & Take out

Contact Information

Web Address

https://www.gabrielasmexicanfood.com/
Face Book URL

https://www.facebook.com/GabrielasCV/
Email: gabrielas.az@outlook.com
Telephone # 928-567-2120

—————————

√ JT's Bistro

348 S. Main St.
Great food, local wine, craft beers
5 star chef. Dine-in, take-out. Pet Friendly outdoor
tables.

Contact Information

Web Address

https://www.jtsbistro.com/
Face Book URL

https://www.facebook.com/Jtbistro/
Email: info@jtsbistro.com
Telephone # 928-567-7520

—————————

La Casita

37 W. Hollamon St.
First-class Mexican cuisine. Serves alcohol.
10A-9P Every Day
Dine-in, on the porch or Take Out available

Contact Information

Face Book URL

https://www.facebook.com/La-
Casita-240420636160416
Telephone # 928-567-3202

—————————

La Fonda Mexican Food

2750 West Horseshoe Bend Dr.
Mexican Food. Take-out, Dine-in
Tue-Sat 11A-8P, Hours 10a-10p Take-Out
Contact Information
Face Book URL
https://www.facebook.com/La-Casita-240420636160416/
Telephone # 928-567-3500

____

Little Caesar's

1673 W. State Route 260
Pizza
Hours 10a-10p Take-Out
Contact Information
Web Address
https://littlecaesars.com/en-us/
Face Book URL
https://www.facebook.com/LittleCaesars
Telephone # 928-567-3165

____

Low Places Bar and Grill

Wingfield Plaza
564 S. Main St. Ste 100
Bar and Grill
Mon-Thur 11-10PM, Fri-Sat 11P-2A
Dine-in, Take-Out
Contact Information
Web Address
https://www.lowplacesbarandgrill.com/
Face Book URL
https://www.facebook.com/LowPlacesCV
Email: shannalee@lowplacesbarandgrill.com
Telephone # 928-567-8722

____

√ Magic Wok

348 S. Main St. Camp Verde, AZ - 86322
Welcome to MAGIC WOK KITCHEN & BAR.
John Teah, Magic Wok Chef and proprietor
invites you to enjoy a truly unique Asian dining
experience. We offer a sensational selection of
seasonal dishes consisting of fresh, locally grown,
hand-selected ingredients.
Hours: Open Thur - Mon 11am - 8pm.
Closed Tue & Wed Sun 11am-5pm
Contact Information
Web Address
https://magicwokaz.com/
Face Book URL
Email: info@magicwokaz.com
Telephone # 928-567-2418

____

McDonald's

1703 Finnie Flat Rd
Open Daily 4A-12A
Take out, drive-through window
Contact Information
Web Address
www.mcdonalds.com
Telephone # 928-567-4388

____

Reserved add space for Chamber adds.

Call to reserve space. Must be a member.

1/4 Page $100, 1/2 Page $200, Full Page $400

Reserved add space for Chamber adds.

Call to reserve space. Must be a member.

1/4 Page $100, 1/2 Page $200, Full Page $400

Reserved add space for Chamber adds.

Call to reserve space. Must be a member.

1/4 Page $100, 1/2 Page $200, Full Page $400

Moscato Italian Restaurant
396 S. Main St.
Gourmet Italian Restaurant
Tue-Sat 11A-9P, Sun 1p-9P, Closed Monday.
Take Out, Eat-in, Outside seating Available
Contact Information
Web Address
https://moscatoazcom.wordpress.com/
Face Book URL
https://www.facebook.com/moscatoitalianaz
Telephone # 928-567-7417

____

Robbies
5155 N. Dave Wingfield Rd. Rimrock
Burgers, cold beer, pizza
Take Out, Dine-In, Outside Dining
11A-8P Daily
Contact Information
Face Book URL
https://www.facebook.com/RobbiesRestaurantAZ/
Email: robbiesrimrock@yahoo.com
Telephone # 928-592-9171

____

Starbucks (Bashas)
650 W. Finnie Flat Road
Coffee, pastries
Hours according to Bashes
Take Out, Eat-In
Contact Information
Web Address
https://www.starbucks.com/
Telephone # 928-567-4585

____

√ Starbucks I-17
1620 State Route 260
Coffee, pastries
4A-8:30P Every Day
Drive Through, Dine-in, Dine on porch
Contact Information
Web Address
https://www.starbucks.com/
Telephone # 928-567-0274

Sonic
350 Castle Lane
Fast Food, burger, Ice cream
Take-out, drive-in window, Dine-In
Contact Information
Web Address
https://www.sonicdrivein.com/
Face Book URL
https://www.facebook.com/sonicdrivein
Telephone # 928-567-7062

____

Subway
In Shell Station
1673 W. Hwy 260
Sandwiches. Hours 730a-930pm, Take-out
Contact Information
Web Address
https://restaurants.subway.com/
Telephone # 928-567-2315

____

Taco Bell
1602 W Hwy 260
Mexican Fast Food
Hours 7A-10P daily
Take out, drive-through window, dine-in
Contact Information
Web Address
locations.tacobell.com
Telephone # 928-554-0233

____

Thai Garden
 3460 E. Beaver Creek Rd. Rimrock
Thai Food. Dine-in, Take-out
Tues-Sun 11A-8:30P
Contact Information
Web Address
www.thaigardenrimrock.com
Telephone # 928-592-9117
928-254-9736

Camp Verde Business-Restaurants

Thanks A Latte

348 Main St. Camp Verde
Sandwiches, coffee
7A-230P Wed- Sunday
Open for Take-Out, dine-in, outside seating
available
Contact Information
Face Book URL
https://www.facebook.com/ThanksALatteCV/
Telephone # 928-567-6450

———————————

Udderly Divine

545 Main St. Camp Verde
Sandwiches, pie, ice cream
7A-5P Closed Sundays
Open for Take-Out, dine-in, outside seating
available.
Contact Information
Face Book URL
https://www.facebook.com/udderlydivine/
Telephone # 928-607-0967

———————————

√ Verde Brewing Co.

 724 N. Industrial Drive Unit 7A
Appetizers, burgers, and craft beer
Inside dining, outside dining, Take-out. 11A-9P
Contact Information
Web Address
https://www.verdebrewing.com/
Telephone # 928-567-8626

Wendy's

1897 Pueblo Ridge Suite C
Burgers, fast food
Take-out, Dine-in, Drive Through window
Contact Information
Web Address
https://www.wendys.com/home
Face Book URL
https://www.facebook.com/wendys/
Telephone # 928-567-9276

———————————

Wingfield Bread Co.

Wingfield Plaza
564 S. Main St.
Fresh Breads, Sandwiches Hours
8A-5P Take-out, walk-in, Dine
Contact Information
Web Address
https://www.wingfieldbread.com/
Face Book URL
https://www.facebook.com/Wingfield-Bread-
Company-284542238384684/
Email: wingfieldbreadco@gmail.com
Telephone # 928-301-9300

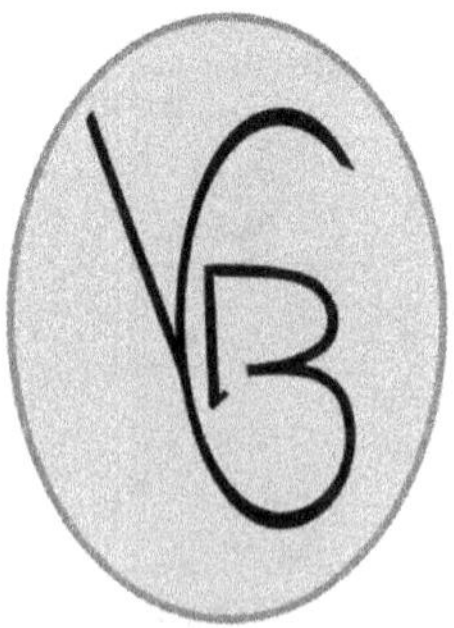

Churches

Asamblea De Dios Aqua Viva
2480 N Arena Del Loma Rd, Camp Verde
Contact Information
Telephone # 928-567-6807

Beaver Creek Baptist Church
3705 E. Beaver Creek Rd.
Our services provide an opportunity for God's
people to both worship Him and to grow in
their walk with Him. Sunday School: Sunday
Morning-9:00 AM, Sunday Worship Services:
Sunday Morning-10:30 AM, Evening Services:
Sunday Evening-6:30 PM
Contact Information
Web Address
https://www.beavercreekbaptistchurch.org/
Face Book URL
https://www.facebook.com/Beaver-Creek-Baptist-
Church-114028198619537
Telephone # 928-567-4557

Calvary Chapel of Camp Verde
Located at: 514 Main Street
Camp Verde AZ. 86322
Mailing Address: PO Box 1374
Camp Verde, AZ. 86322
Non-denominational Bible Church. Children's
programs and Sunday school.
Sun Services 8, 10, Wed 6:30PM.
Contact Information
Web Address
https://www.calvarychapelcv.com/
Face Book URL
https://www.facebook.com/campverdebaptist
Email: email: calvarycvaz@calvarychapel.com
Telephone # 928-567-2171

Camp Verde Baptist Church
299 E Hollamon St
We are a family of Christ-followers dedicated
to proclaiming the fullness of the gospel to
Camp Verde, Arizona and participating in Acts
1:8 missions around the world. We are committed
to the study of the Bible and living out its
teachings in every aspect of our lives. Wherever
you are on your own faith journey, we welcome
you to join us as we explore the grace of God
together
Sunday: Sunday School– 9:30 AM to 10:45 AM,
Worship Service– 11:00 AM to 12:00 PM, Nursery
Provided Every Sunday Morning– 11:00 AM to
12:00 PM, Bible Study– 6:00 PM to 7:00 PM.
Contact Information
Web Address
https://www.campverdebaptist.com/
Face Book URL
https://www.facebook.com/campverdebaptist
Telephone # 928-567-3324

Camp Verde Christian Assembly
280 Camp Lincoln Road
Contact Information
Telephone # 928-634-4321

Camp Verde Christian Church
621 Howards Rd
Camp Verde, Az. 86322
Mailing Address PO Box 766 Camp Verde Az.
86322.
Non denominational Bible Church established in
1975. Solid biblical teaching. Fellowship hour at
10am the first Sunday of every month.
Sunday Services 10:30am Pastor Greg Young
presiding. Check out the online sermons!
Contact Information
Web Address
https://www.campverdechristian.church
Email: campverdechristianchurch@gmail.com

Reserved add space for Chamber adds.

Call to reserve space. Must be a member.

1/4 Page $100, 1/2 Page $200, Full Page $400

Camp Verde Community Church

661 Howards Rd suite A

Contact Information

Web Address

https://www.cvcommunitychurch.org/

Face Book URL

https://www.facebook.com/
CampVerdeCommunityChurch?fref=ts

Email: campverdecommunitychurch@gmail.com

Telephone # 928-567-3447

____

Church of Jesus Christ of Latter Day Saints

360 South 5th St.

Contact Information

Web Address

https://www.churchofjesuschrist.org/?lang=eng

Face Book URL

https://www.facebook.com/ChurchofJesusChrist/

Telephone # 928-567-3206

____

Church of Christ-Verde Valley

2001 N. Arena Del Loma

At the Verde Valley Church of Christ we are a
spiritual family united in our Lord Jesus Christ.
We are a non-denominational Christian family.
Not Catholic, Protestant or Jewish. Just Christian,
teaching New Testament Christianity as taught
2000 years ago.

Sunday Schedule: Bible Classes – 9:30 am,
Worship – 10:30 am, Evening Worship – 6:00 pm,
Wednesday Schedule: Bible Classes – 7:00 pm

Contact Information

Web Address

http://verdevalleychurchofchrist.org/

Email: admin@verdevalleychurchofchrist.org

Telephone # 928-567-5317

____

Desert Willow Church Assembly of God

918 State Highway 260

Mail; PO Box 4287

Camp Verde, Az 86322

The First Assembly of God is a place for families
to prosper emotionally and spiritually. We care
about every person that enters through the doors of
our church. We believe with God that all things are
possible and that with His help we can accomplish
anything. There are many ways for you to hear the
Word of God for any age.

Contact Information

Web Address

https://desertwillowchurch.org/

Face Book URL

https://www.facebook.com/Desert-Willow-
Church-114585860724888

Telephone # 928-567-0451 (Office)

651-210-8577 (Pastor Kent)

____

Freedom Assembly of God

4810 E Beaver Creek Rd, Rimrock

Meets at Beaver Creek Elementary School

Contact Information

Telephone # 928-899-3895 or 928-567-3568

____

Camp Verde Business-Churches

Grace Community Lutheran Church

5100 N. Stevens Dr ,Rimrock
A small, but friendly group of believers. Faith building sermons. Family style fellowship lunches. Welcoming to the community. Stands firm on the Bible. Shares the love of Christ with all!

Contact Information

Face Book URL
https://www.facebook.com/
Gracecommunitylutheran
Email: msstude@yahoo.com
Telephone # 928-567-4608

____

Lighthouse Baptist Church

348 S. Main Ste #7
Friendly people, knowledgeable pastor, Bible based teaching. Sunday AM 11:00 and Evening at 6:00, Wed at 6:00PM

Contact Information

Web Address
https://www.lighthousebaptistchurchcv.org/
Email: donrandall11@gmail.com
Telephone # 928-634-1008

____

√ Middle Verde Rock Church

2221 W. Reservation Loop Rd.
Middle Verde Rock Church is a Baptist Mission that reaches out to the local native American population, Rainbow Acres, a Ranch for persons with Developmental Disabilities, and the assorted persons in Camp Verde, AZ, and the surrounding communities. Donations are accepted with our thanks and as a non-profit, are tax-deductible. Sunday Rancher Service 9 am Sunday Service 10:45 am Wednesday Evening Service 6 pm

Contact Information

Web Address
https://www.mvrockchurch.org/
Face Book URL
https://www.facebook.com/
mvrockchurch/?modal=admin_todo_tour
Email: drjwwatson@suddenlink.net
Telephone # 928-554-0232

____

Montezuma Chapel

3450 E. Rusty Spur Rd.
Montezuma Chapel is a Jesus-centered, Bible-focused non-denominational faith community striving to grow and to share Christ's love to all people.

Contact Information

Face Book URL
https://www.facebook.com/Montezuma-Chapel-367110826666289/
Email: montezuma.chapel@gmail.com
Telephone # 928-567-4804

____

Camp Verde Business-Churches

New Beginnings Church of Nazarene

644 S. 7th Street
We welcome visitors to New Beginnings Church of the Nazarene Tuesday - Friday: 10:00 AM - 1:00 PM Closed: Monday and Saturday
Sunday: Bible Study at 9:30 AM, Worship at 10:45 AM

Contact Information

Web Address
https://newbeginningsnaz.com/
Face Book URL
https://www.facebook.com/newbeginningsCV/
Email: reflectionsofgrace@msn.com
Telephone # 928-567-9336

____

Parkside Church

401 Camp Lincoln
Parkside is pressing on in our vision to inspire Christ-centered Gospel-driven living through Biblical worship, discipleship, and community. We will keep posting sermons, worship videos, and other resources and we are here to help meet the needs of our Parkside family and our community.

Contact Information

Web Address
https://www.parksidecampverde.com/
Face Book URL
https://www.facebook.com/ParksideChurchCV/
Email: info@parksidecampverde.com
Telephone # 928-567-3577

____

St. Frances Cabrini Catholic Church

781 Cliffs Parkway, Camp Verde
St. Frances Cabrini Church, like our namesake, St. Frances Cabrini herself, has been a vigorous and an apostolic church. We build, we teach, we celebrate and we worship. We carved away our rocky hillside and planted rose bushes. We offer the sacraments in Spanish and we continue to provide a Catholic continuity and community to those many new pioneers who have moved to Camp Verde from all around the world. We have been having regular daily Mass her at St. Frances Cabrini at 9A, Mon-Sat and also at 9A Sundays.

Contact Information

Face Book URL
https://www.facebook.com/pages/St%20 Frances%20Cabrini%20Catholic%20 Church/143959002316359/
Telephone # 928-567-3543

____

Seventh Day Adventist Church

1406 N. Boot Hill Dr.
Good News for the Camp Verde Congregation. Our new pastor, Mike Ortel comes to us from the Glendale Church. You can find out a lot about what is happening in our church by checking out the pages on our website.

Contact Information

Web Address
http://campverde22.adventistchurchconnect.org/
Telephone # PH 928-567-4281
Mike Ortel, Pastor: 704-651-3052

____

Camp Verde Chamber Resource 2021-22 INDEX

Business	Page
Family Dollar x2	74/130
Fasteen Farms	118
FD Creative Designs	118
Feldmeier Properties/Central AZ Cons	140
Ferrell Gas	21/97
Filberto's	97
Firebird Towing	98
Fiscor Heating and Cooling	130
Fit-In-15	80
Flew the Coop Nashville Hot Chicken Shack	98
Footwork Auto License and Title	27
Fort River Auto Glass	59
Fort Verde Laundromat	15/59
Fort Verde State Historical Park	59
Fort Verde Suites	59
Franklin Pest Control	80/140
Freedom Assembly of God	157
French's RV Center	118
Fresh Focuses Photography	140
Friends of the Verde River	141
Full-Line Striping	141

G

Business	Page
Gabriela's	98
Gardner's Recycling	119
Get Hitched Kwick	59
Glorybound Publishing	60
Go West Design Co.	119
Good 2 Go in Chevron Station	22
Goettls High Desert Mechanical HVAC & Plumbing Specialists	119
Grace Community Lutheran Church	158
Grant's Appliance Repair	141
Graves Propane	22
Green River Hauling LLC	141
Groome Transportation	26
Guide to Recycling	18

H

Business	Page
Hair by Maya	60
Hammes Surveying LLC	119
Hand Helping Handiman	119
Hanna's Nails	74
Hansen Enterprises Fleet Repair LLC	120
Harvey's Roofing LLC	131
Hauser & Hauser Farms	80
Hauser Family Cook Book	81
Hauser Glass Inc	98
Haven Health of Camp Verde	44/99
Heartlinks Woodworks	131
Heritage Land Surveying	60
High Country Power Washing	141
Hillside Canine Resort and Spa	99
Hollamon Generations RD Boring	60
Hope Women's Center	8/38/60
Home Smart Elite	81
Huges Net- Satellite	20
Hugh-Mac Transport	120

I

Business	Page
Independent Vital Life LLC	99
Inge's Uniquely Warm Caring Home	99
Illegal Street Wear	142
Inspired Gunworks LLC	61
Institute for Vibrant Living	99
Insurer's Network LTD.	61
Integrated Therapeutic Mobile Massage	61
Integrity Auto Ts Auto & Diesel Repair	100

J

Business	Page
J & J Machine & Tool	100
Jackpot Ranch	87
Jim's Trading Post	131
Joel Westervelt Architect	61
John Graves Propane of Arizona Inc	100
Johnny Rockets	87
Jone's Ford Verde Valley	27/120
Jones Ford Verde Valley Rental Cars	27
Jordan's Heavy Duty Towing	100
Joshua Tree Landscape	62
JT's Bistro	61

K

Business	Page
Kaisen Collision Center	23/120
Kathy Tryon Mary Kay Cosmetics	142
Kilby & Sons Construction	81
Kiwanis Camp Verde	62
Kiwanis International Clothes Closet	131
KM Drilling Inc.	142
Kocisko Construction	62
KP Ventures Well Drilling & Pump Co	121
Krazy K RV Park	81

L

Business	Page
LC Studio Hair and Nails	81
La Casita	62
La Fonda Mexican Food	121
Laid Back Jewelry	62
Lighthouse Baptist Church	159
Ligon Excavation Inc	121
Little Caesar's	100
Lori's Lookin Good Hair Design	63
Los Zpote's	74
Love Yourself Love Your Health	81
Low Places Bar and Grill	63
Lucas Tactical Manufacturing	63
Lucas Tactical & Pawn	63

M

Business	Page
MJP Electric Inc	101
MJP Contractors LLC	101
MSP Drywall LLC	143
Magic Wok	63
Magnolia Beauty Bar	132
Majestic Flooring LLC	83
Main Street Studios	63
Mamaw's Laundry	25
Manife Mini Storage	100
Mario and Mario Landscaping	142
Manzanita Outreach Food Sharing	38
Maverick	75
McDonald's	100
McDonald Brothers Construction	101
Mcquireville Minimart	132

Business	Page
Medicare Solutions	64
Melode's Grooming	64
Memories IT	64
Metropolis Support LLC	88
MGG Cleaning Service	142
Michelle Lee Photography	64
Middle Verde Rock Church	159
Minute Mart #48 In Shell Station	22
Montana Mercantile	101
Montezuma Appliance Repair	132
Montezuma Chapel	158
Montezuma Family Dental	132
Montezuma Reality	83
Montezuma Rimrock Fire Department (Copper Canyon Fire Department)	9
Montezuma Veterinary Service	64
Moscato Italian Restaurant	153
Mountain Springs Buffet	88
Mower Medic	83/88
Mr. Rooter Plumbing	64
Mulcaire & Son Contracting LLC	101
Music in the Stacks	38
Mystic Muse	64

N

Business	Page
NACOG North Az Coun of Govt EWD	143
NAPA Auto Parts	24/39/75
NRL Mortgage	65
Nails by Dani	64
Nashwa Farms	144
National Bank of Arizona	75
NaturMed Inc.	101
New Beginnings Church of Nazarene	159
New Life Thrift and Gift	64
New Trails Expansion in Camp Verde	39
NextCare Urgent Care - Cottonwood	10
Nice Jon's Inc	101
Noguez Farm	83
North Horizon Plumbing	102
Northern Arizona Healthcare Immediate Care – Camp Verde	9

Name	Page
Northern Arizona Mold Inspector	102
Northern Arizona Pump Inc.	133
Northern Hardscape LLC	102
O	
Old World Guns	66
On the Go Auto Repair	103
Oothoudt Brothers Inc	103
O'Reilly Auto Parts	24/75
Osher Life Long Learning Institute	29
Out of Africa	122
P	
P & C Electric	122
PJ Carson Acoustic Music	66
Painless Stitches Upholstery	103
Parkside Church	159
Parker Construction Enterprise	103
Patriot Disposal	17
Peejay Plumbing Heating & Fire	103
Pete Clark Auto Repair	23/66
Petmec Plumbing Solutions	133
Petrie Contracting LLC	103
PIEH Tool Company Inc.	104
Pierce Builders LLC	104
Phillip England Center for the Performing Arts	40/83
Plowing Ahead Ranch	104
Poison Control	10
Prescott Nat Forest Verde Ranger Dist	10
Protection Orders	11
Q	
Quintus Inc	104
R	
R & K Custom Homes	105
Rainbow Acres	88
Rancho Verde RV Park LLC	120
Rask Construction	133
Raul's Hair Salon LLC	66
Rayburn Electric LLC	105
Rays Of Sunshine Center Inc.	84
Razor's Edge Hair Salon	66
Remick Law PLC	105
Renovare Wellness Center	84
Rimrock Resale shoppe	133
Rimrock Super Storage	134
Rise N' Shine House Cleaning	105
Road Runner Rentals	105
Rob Witt, Arizona Prime Real Estate	33
Robbies	124
Robinson Golf Cars	105
Rocky Construction Excavation	105
Roto-Fab LLC	106
Route 66 Images	106
Ruby Road Resale Mall	106
S	
Safetree PPE	112
St Francis of Cabrini Catholic Church	159
Saint Vincent De Paul	66
Salon PhD Professional Hair Designers LLC	67
Salt Mine Wine	106
Scott Brothers Drywall INC	88
Sedona CanAm Rentals	144
Seekins Enterprises	106
Select Net Autos	67
Seventh Day Adventist Church	159
Sinagua Malt	107
Small Engine Repair	134
Snap Fitness	75
Solid Rock Tile	66
Sonic	84
South Verde High School	29
Southwest Tank and Steel Inc.	122
Sparklight	20
Specialty Powder Coating	107
Spectrum Health Services	45/76
Spot Masters	25
Stallings Performance Horse	107
Starbucks (Bashes) and I-17	76/108

Verde Valley Internet LLC	145
Verde Valley Kayaker's Club	41
Verde Valley Medical Center	11
Verde Valley Medical Clinic	46
Verde Valley Resale	70
Verde Valley Sanctuary	12/41/70
Verde View Senior Apartments	47
Viasat-Satellite	21
Vortex ATV Rentals	146

W-X

Walgreens Drug Store	78
Waste Management Yavapai	19
WD Automotives LLC	124
West Direct Oil	124
Wendy's	111
Westcott Funeral Home	72
Wingfield Bread Company	72

Y

Yaquis Taqueria	146
Yavapai-Apache Sand & Rock	125
Yavapai Apache Health Center	46
Yavapai Apache Police Department	12
Yavapai Apache Fry Bread and Jewelry	89
Yavapai Apache Whitehills	111
Yavapai College SBDC	29/146
Yavapai County Jail	12
Yavapai County Sheriff's Department	16/42
Yavapai Fence	125
Yavapai Title Agency	72
Your Neighborhood Handiman	111

Z

Zane Grey RV Village	114
Zane Grey Storage	114
Zuks Off Road	114

Camp Verde Chamber & Business Alliance
522 Finnie Flat Rd. Ste E 179 Camp Verde, AZ 86322
www.campverde.biz
cvcbacampverde@gmail.com
928-203-6863

Mission Statement: The **Camp Verde Chamber & Business Alliance (**CVBA) is a dynamic network dedicated to the prosperity of businesses-new and old, small or large--in Camp Verde and throughout the Verde Valley. We honor the rich heritage of our community and enthusiastically support future development. We are committed to provide representation, promotion, and resources for the business community.

BENEFITS OF MEMBERSHIP

→ **Business is flagged** on the website as member.
→ **3 month picture advertising** on www.campverde.biz web site in area available. (Open soon)
→ **Option to purchase** additional picture advertising slots for quarter, half and full page.
→ **Schedule Ribbon Cutting Ceremony** with Mayor of the Town of Camp Verde and CVCBA Board Member with promotional video which is put on the Home Page of the www.campverde.biz web site, flyers and pr in local newspaper.
→ **Schedule Open House** with invitation to CVCBA with submission of photos and/or video. CVCBA will send out blanket business e-mails to all local businesses (on our list). 1-per year.
→ **Special Promotions**. Tell us what is going on, and we will publicize it. Will be included in monthly e-mail blast. Limit 1 per quarter.
→ **Mixers** held at local restaurants where businesses can interact with one another.
→ **CVCBA Meetings** will be scheduled along the way. We release date and time by email to our members and on the front of the website.

     √ **Meet and Greet** other local businesses.
     √ **Down to Business** 20 Min (Learn about a topic presented by a local business owner.)
     √ **Professional Business Strategy**- 20 Min taught by Business Professional Assistance Options
        outside of Camp Verde--Importing Education.
     √ **Educate Local**-taught by *Member or Partner*. It is an extension of either Down to Business
        or Professional Business Strategy. This is for material which needs greater detail than
        option of 20 min during CVCBA will allow. Generally, these classes hinge on Down to
        Business session of similar topic. Class is 45min-1.45 min and given prior to the CVCBA
        meeting on the same day.

Cost of membership is $75 per year, beginning on July 1st. Entrance is divided by quarter and then yearly. Your membership will be an active partnership with the Camp Verde Chamber & Business Alliance and as such requires active participation on various initiative work groups and meetings. By applying for membership, you are accepting responsibility for participation. CVCBA reserves the right to rescind membership if acceptance is found to have been based on false information, or other action or practices which may conflict with CVCBA's purpose and by-laws. Membership dues are $75 per year for Partners and free to Associate Partners. Dues are quarterly upon initial payment and due June 1 thereafter. Please see CVBA By-Laws for details on the rights and responsibilities of Membership.

CAMP VERDE CHAMBER APPLICATION

The Camp Verde Chamber & Business Alliance (CVBA) is a dynamic network dedicated to the prosperity of businesses-new and old, small or large--in Camp Verde and throughout the Verde Valley. We honor the rich heritage of our community and enthusiastically support future development. We are committed to provide representation, promotion, and resources for the business community.

Application for Partner (Business)

Associate Partner (Individual)

Reciprocal Partner (Non-Profit)

Name(s)

Business Name

Mailing Address

Business Phone

Email Address

What is the nature of your business?

Sole Proprietor

LLC

Other

Business License Number (If Applicable)

Physical Address

Cell Phone

Web and/or FaceBook Address

Your membership will be an active partnership with the Camp Verde Chamber & Business Alliance and as such requires active participation on various initiative work groups and meetings. By applying for membership, you are accepting responsibility for participation. CVCBA reserves the right to rescind membership if acceptance is found to have been based on false information, or other action or practices which may conflict with CVCBA's purpose and by-laws. Membership dues are $75 per year for Partners and Associate Partners. Reciprocal Partners fees are waved. Dues are yearly Jan 1. Please see CVCBA By-Laws for details on the rights and responsibilities of Membership. CVCBA is a non-profit business registered in the State of Arizona.

Signature

Date

Payment Amount $ √   ⊡

Card #

VVi   EXP

Camp Verde Chamber & Business Alliance 2021-22

$75 per year for Partners
$75 per year for Associate Partners
$0 Non-Profit (Reciprocal)

The Camp Verde Chamber Business Resource

This book is a compilation taken from the Camp Verde Chamber website originally compiled in the middle of COVID by several individuals. One of the requests made to the Chamber was to have a complete business resource. We accepted this challenge and embarked on an adventure to locate as much information related to businesses as possible.

Colleen, Paul, and Sheri drove around to locate off-the-grid businesses and looked on Google to learn additional information. Then, we accessed their websites and Facebook sites, called their stores, and spoke to them directly to learn of their services. Dana worked tirelessly on the 2022-23 edition.

We opted to park the site on GoDaddy to make it easy to access using a desktop or a phone. John and Dana were instrumental in compiling data. We gathered and gathered from all of the sources available. Up to this date, we have made every attempt to list viable active businesses in storefronts and home-based collecting their 'service list' from their own FaceBook or web pages.

The Camp Verde Chamber & Business Alliance has used business logos (where apt) and copied services and numbers which are publicly accessible. We are not liable for the services which are advertised by the businesses; we simply copied what they said that they do. Suppose any business has changed its services and contact information. In that case, we encourage them to let us know through the contact page on our website. The updates will be released in the next printing of this compilation.

Compilation of the Camp Verde Chamber Business Resource was under the direction of Glorybound Publishing and Sheri Hauser.
For the most updated information on businesses, please consult the Chamber Website at www.campverde.biz.

Camp Verde Chamber Resource:

Emergency
Move to Camp Verde
Community Resources
Business
Downtown
  Finnie Flat
  Montezuma Hwy
  Hwy 260 East of I17
  Hwy 260 West of I17
  Rimrock
  Surrounding Areas
Restaurants
Churches
Chamber

Verde Valley Tourism Guide:

Campgrounds & Picnic Areas
Trailheads & Horse Trails
Visit the Sites
Vineyards & Breweries
Air BnB
Retreats
Sedona
  Hotels in Sedona
  Tourism in Sedona